HOW LONG?
The Trek through the Wilderness

BY PATRICK ODEN

BARCLAY PRESS
Newberg, Oregon

How Long?
The Trek through the Wilderness

© 2011 by Patrick Oden

Published by
Barclay Press
211 N. Meridian St., #101
Newberg, OR 97132
800.962.4014
www.barclaypress.com

ISBN 978-1-59498-023-7

All rights reserved.
No part of this publication may be reproduced, stored in a retrieval system, or transmitted in any form or by any means—for example, electronic, photocopy, recording—without the prior written permission of the publisher. The only exception is brief quotations in printed reviews.

All Scripture quotations, unless otherwise noted, are taken from the *Holy Bible, New International Version*®. *NIV*®. Copyright © 1973, 1978, 1984 by Biblica, Inc.™ Used by permission of Zondervan. All rights reserved worldwide. www.zondervan.com.

Scripture quotations marked *NRSV* are taken from *The New Revised Standard Version*, copyright 1989, 1995 by the Division of Christian Education of the National Council of the Churches of Christ in the United States of America. Used by permission. All rights reserved.

Cover design by Darryl Brown

Acknowledgments & Dedication

Every so often someone asks me about the setting and characters of my first book, *It's a Dance: Moving with the Holy Spirit*. It's a fictional setting, but rarely is any work wholly fiction. People want to know if I'm Nate or any of the other characters, or how much my own church experiences went into the details of what happens in the book. My answer is that no, I'm not Nate, or any of the other characters, though there's a lot of me that is in Nate, and many of my experiences do show up in the questions and issues I discuss. But  it's not really about me. When I write I have in mind real people, real stories, real questions, and I attempt to mix these into a cohesive whole. The same is true for this present work. The setting is the same, but the experiences of the characters are quite different. In *It's a Dance* I created an idealist community in order to explore the work of the Spirit. *How Long?* is a little more honest, in a way, pointing out that life lived in community with God is not a constant song and dance. Indeed, every life encounters great difficulties, some of which are very hard to understand. And the difficulties are often strongest when we are faced with holding onto our faith when we see there's nothing to hold onto anymore.

This reality is "the wilderness." My own times of wilderness are not always filled with hope, to be sure, so I am absolutely thankful for those men and women who remind me about the hope that is truly found in God. Much of my hope during these wilderness times comes from reading the writings of men and women long dead on this present earth, but still alive in Christ and in their resonating message.

My parents, who have gone through many wilderness experiences, constantly remind me to hold on. They not only encourage me, they believe in me, and our many conversations over the years became like the food the ravens brought Elijah during his time in the Kerith Ravine (1 Kings 17:2-6). I cannot put my love and appreciation for them into words.

My brother, Jon, and my friend Peter stand out to me as well. Though our conversations have not been constant, their friendship over the years has been a constant blessing in my life. Both have been in places of shadow and darkness, and both have found their way back to hope, following the light, hearing the music, being faithful in their steps. They remind me that God does work. God is working.

I also want to thank Dr. Veli-Matti Kärkkäinen. His encouragement, guidance, and investment in my work has been immensely valuable. My understanding of theology, ministry, and the work of God in this world has been profoundly impacted by his teaching and direction. I am proud to be his student and I look forward to many years of learning together, during my present studies and long after I graduate.

My most recent wilderness experience lasted quite a while. I lost hope at times. I felt darkness overwhelm me. But I continued forward, because I heard music playing far in the distance. Over the last few years, this music became much more clear. As I continued to walk in the wilderness, God seemed to lead me toward an oasis, and in this oasis I heard a woman singing and playing a guitar. She was singing words to God, and singing with all her soul. I asked her if she would dance with me. She replied, "Of course." She reminds me every day to continue to hope, to continue to seek, to continue to dance. Our hope is not in vain. Because God does work. And when he does? Wow.

This book—this book of looking for hope in the midst of wilderness—is dedicated to her, my wife, the love of my life, my best friend, Amy.

Contents

1. Introduction \ 1
2. When good answers aren't there \ 7
3. When doubts and questions abound \ 13
4. When that unsettled feeling hangs on \ 31
5. When 'being' trumps 'doing' \ 45
6. When bad times hit good people \ 61
7. When it's time to let go \ 75
8. When God hears the cries of his people \ 91
9. When all hope is gone \ 107
10. When God calls \ 131
11. When it's one step forward and two steps back \ 153
12. When you can't see a way out \ 171
13. When milk is not enough \ 189
14. When cowards take charge \ 209
15. When a friend walks away \ 231
16. When God deals with slow learners \ 241

1

introduction

Nate Shipley woke up early. Instead of the usual sound of steady traffic, he heard only the song of the occasional mockingbird. He anticipated a few hours dedicated to writing; a well-known Christian magazine had invited him to contribute an article. His efforts apparently resonated in important circles.

Just write about your community, they said.

They gave him an opportunity, a chance to spread the message a bit farther. He didn't want to think of it this way, but he couldn't help it. The thought made him smile. Faces, names, and stories flooded his mind.

God had been doing a work. Nate joined in on part of that—just a part, even if he seemed to be the leader. It was God's work, with the Holy Spirit bringing amazing people to join in, making the community go way beyond anything Nate had imagined five years before. Back then, he left his job at Crestview Community Church to become a janitor at a downtown restaurant and began to serve in a leadership role for a new kind of Christian community hosted at the same location. So much had happened. After thirty years of being a Christian, ten of these in full-time ministry, Nate truly met Jesus in the context of this very non-traditional Christian community.

His heart felt open and free; he even felt relaxed in his work even though so much required his attention. Instead of feeling as if life pressed down on him, he felt life provided opportunities to celebrate. He also knew it was the Spirit's work, not his own.

Even after all the time since leaving that old world behind, his heart felt strangely warm. He felt more than his own excitement. And the feeling went deeper than the large, half-finished mug of French roast sitting beside him could provide. God really works.

To be sure, more than his emotions changed with this christological encounter. While he never wore a suit and tie in his ministry work, he certainly did affect the casual pastor's look for a long while. Back when he persevered in traditional churches he owned quite a collection of Dockers and polo shirts to go with his short—but not too short—conservatively combed hair. Now? He shaved once a week or so, if he remembered, mostly because of the itching. He wore his hair longer, finding a scattered wavy pattern that seemed to change style every day. Mostly he wore jeans on cold days and shorts on hot days, almost always with his Tevas. He no longer owned any polos. A collection of T-shirts reflected his mood day by day—some with art, some with cartoons, some just a solid color or a curious design. He became familier with the thrift stores within walking distance. Every so often he gathered the shirts he hadn't worn in a while and traded them in. He stood taller than average, a little over six feet, but his waistline lost a few inches. Thirty pounds makes a difference. This new life led to better dietary habits.

Nate lost his house and his fiancée. This road to finding peace occasionally frustrated, confused, and angered him. It involved giving up so much and taking up so much. The hours of prayer and study and conversation seemed endless. He sacrificed time and energy with almost entirely no practical benefit—except for the joy.

Maybe there's really nothing more practical than joy.

"That's the theme," he said out loud. A pigeon on the ledge outside his window cooed in response. *A sign.* He laughed. Then he remembered that the dove is the symbol, not a pigeon, and he laughed again as he tried to figure out what image a city pigeon suggested.

Searching for joy is what initially led him to leave his staff position at a large suburban church and think about starting something new. Prayer with close friends gave him new inspiration. But things really began to change when, out of the blue, he received an offer to manage a restaurant. When the friend of Nate's brother died in an accident, his father was faced with selling his life's work or finding someone who would run the business for him. Nate was surprised, to say the least, when Carlos asked him if he wanted the restaurant, and the building, for not only a restaurant but also a space for his new church.

God worked. And continued to work. The prayers didn't stop. As Nate and a group of people who shared his vision began to settle into their new space, they realized how the Spirit already worked, and they sought this work—work that did not seem to always match what people expected when they thought of the Spirit. Studying Scripture surprised them all: the formal teaching they had in church and elsewhere left out a great deal of the work of the Spirit as it was revealed in the Bible. The Spirit does not put on a show and does not exist merely to add rhetorical flair to theological talks.

The Spirit, Nate realized, leads people to Jesus. The Spirit draws people into community and breaks down the artificial barriers created between sacred and secular. God works everywhere, after all, even if people do not recognize or acknowledge that work. The Spirit empowers holiness and continually encourages God's followers to welcome strangers—people who aren't strangers to God. He even loves them! The Spirit spurs people to give, incites creativity of all kinds, and provokes this creativity to become realized within the community—though not necessarily, or even primarily, in a Sunday morning service. The Spirit leads the church as a body, and unites the community in time and space with others who worship God.

Realizing these works—acting on these—led Nate to see the fruits of the Spirit all around. Joy and peace grew. People relaxed, even as many questions remained unanswered. Nate met Jesus and began to really sit with him. He gathered with others—men and women committed to each other and committed to their community of Pasadena—reaching out and reaching deep with the Good News that Christ offers, not only in word but also in action. This became the meat of what he hoped to share through his writing.

Two thousand words into the article and two more mugs of French roast. The sun began to shine through the branches of the tree across the street and into his window. Traffic drowned out the sound of the exuberantly singing sparrows and finches. The pigeon had flown away an hour earlier.

This is good, he thought, thinking of both the article and his life.

He got up and stood by the window, composed his thoughts for an inspiring conclusion. A flash of brilliance made him smile, and so he sat back down before he lost the words in his head. He moved the mouse to the formatting menu. The cursor froze. He tapped the space bar. Nothing. Moved the mouse again. Nothing. Stared at the screen. Nothing. Went to the bathroom and came back. The cursor still wouldn't move. Everything was frozen. Thank God for autosave, he thought, while reaching down and manually turning off the computer. The LCD went blank. Then it brightened again, more than usual. A bright blue with a couple paragraphs of technobabble.

He restarted the computer. Same thing.

The sound of Beethoven's "Moonlight" sonata began to fill the room. Nate reached into his backpack and opened his cell.

"Yeah," he answered, vaguely irritated.

"Nate," Luis responded, "We need you at Huntington Hospital. Melissa...."

"What happened?"

"Nate, last night she was attacked. Robbed. Who knows what else."

"How is she?"

"They don't know, Nate. She's been shot. They don't know. I just found out. I'm on my way myself."

"Leaving right now."

Nate folded his cell phone, grabbed his Dodgers hat, and turned off the computer again. The article, whatever was left of it, didn't matter. He put on his sandals and a clean shirt, giving no thought to showering or shaving.

His feet rattled the old, wooden, white-washed stairs and then he quickly pushed open the back door to the small parking lot where he, a couple of waitresses, and the manager parked. There was no room for anyone else.

Nate froze in the doorway. There were no cars in the lot. He stared at the spot by the dirty, dented blue dumpster where he was sure he had parked his car the night before.

Two pigeons strutted around the asphalt. A pile of broken glass—lit by the sun now rising over the fence—caught his eye. Broken glass where he knew he had parked his car last night.

Nate remained motionless, as if time had stopped.

One of the pigeons cooed.

Why did God let this happen?

Is God still in charge?

2

when good answers aren't there

"Thanks for picking me up," Nate says as he opens Debbie's car door. He notices her red and puffy eyes, which, along with her dark hair, make her skin look almost sickly pale. Her hair is wet and only quickly combed. Debbie Langlo is usually put together and stylish, sometimes more so than her job as a waitress at the Columba requires. Not this morning. She hasn't put on any makeup and she's wearing what she calls her "hanging-out" shorts, baggy and beige, with a white, oversized T-shirt. She was just getting out of the shower when she got the call and didn't have any thought about spending more time getting ready—a sure sign of the seriousness of the moment.

"No problem," she responds. "Did you call the police about your car?"

"Yeah, after I talked to you. I said I'd go to the station later to fill out a report."

"Bad day."

"Seems like it."

"Have you heard anything?" Debbie asks. "About the car?"

"Melissa?"

"No. I haven't talked to anyone besides you or Luis. Have you heard anything?"

"No," Debbie says as she makes a left onto Fair Oaks Avenue. "Why, Nate? Why did this happen?"

"I don't know any of the details."

"No! Why did God let this happen?"

"I don't know. I honestly don't know. I mean, I can preach a whole sermon on this. Why bad things happen. But right now? Words don't fit. They're empty. I don't know."

"Maybe we can't know," Debbie says. "Maybe there's no reason. I don't know, Nate, but I need to. Even though I know I likely won't. I don't know what to do with this."

"It's too early still. We just need to get to the hospital. There's way too much going on here for us to think we'd have the complete package of answers. Not like this."

"Yeah. It's too early."

"There is one thing I do know, Debbie."

"What's that?"

"God is still in charge."

"What does that mean? Sometimes, Nate, you say too much. Don't be a pastor, Nate. Don't give me that Christian soothing to help calm my delicate soul. How dare you? Don't be like that."

"Sorry, I was just...."

"You should have stopped at 'I don't know.' I don't want to hear the vague Christianese. I know those words. They don't mean anything. Not really. Not with something like this."

Debbie and Nate pull into the parking lot.

"'God is in charge,'" Debbie scoffs. "How does that help? If God is in charge, Nate, why are we here now? Does God want Melissa hurt or dead? If he's in charge, then it sure seems like that's what he wants. What kind of 'in-charge' God would have us here? Don't answer that, Nate. Let's just go inside."

Nate opens the car door and stands up but doesn't move. Just stands as still as the small oak sapling next to him. Right now—for some reason—he really misses Stacy, his ex-fiancée. He hasn't felt that for a while. She was always good in a crisis. Maybe that's why she started so many.

"Nate, come on," Debbie says, walking back to the car. "Sorry I got mad. It's just…."

"I know. I'm sorry too. I guess I want answers. Any answers. I don't like the thought that maybe there aren't any."

"Life is like that," Debbie says, then walks over and hugs Nate. "Go through enough crap and you learn there just aren't answers to everything, even if you really want them and really need them. They're just not there. Not the way we want, at least."

"I guess not."

"You're here. I'm here. Others are here. That's enough answers for me right now, you know? That's enough."

"Hey!" a man yells at them from across the parking lot as he steps out of a red Prius. Nate and Debbie stop and turn. The man waves, shuts his car door, and jogs toward them.

"Hey, Luke," Nate says, when the man draws closer. Luke, the newly promoted editor of the *Southern California Clarion*, a Pasadena-based newspaper focusing on local issues and goings-on, is dressed well—a lot nicer than Debbie or Nate—but still within "California casual." He wears his button-down striped shirt open at the collar and untucked from his dark gray dress pants. His pants, and very nice black dress shoes are the only indications that he could transform quickly to a more demanding environment. Luke and his wife, Heather, joined with Nate and the others after Luke was assigned to write articles on local churches and came across the Columba. Part of Luke's research included visiting their weekly gathering and meeting others involved. Doing that not only produced an article but also a personal spiritual resurgence. After a few cautious weeks Luke and Heather decided to leap into what was going on.

"What have you heard?" Luke asks, a little out of breath.

"Not too much," Debbie answers. "Not enough. You?"

"Heather told me Melissa's in surgery now," Luke replies. "She didn't have too many other details. She's on her way now. Since I was so close, I thought I should come right away."

They hurry through the automatic doors and take the elevator to the third floor.

*"But I cry to you for help,
O Lord; in the morning my
prayer comes before you.
Why, O Lord, do you reject me
and hide your face from me?"*

(Psalm 88:13-14)

3

when doubts and questions abound

"Have I ever told you about the dreams I had when I was young?" Melissa asks. She leans up a little in her hospital bed as she speaks. A week has passed since the shooting.

"About becoming an artist?" Debbie responds.

"No, not my dreams for what I would do. My dreams when I would fall asleep. My real dreams."

"No, you've never told me."

"I had bunches and bunches. Almost every night for a long time. Sometimes when I woke up in the middle of the night after having one of those dreams, I'd turn on my light, and then draw the image. I had a whole sketchbook filled with drawings. Some I would color later, some I wouldn't."

"All the while you were growing up?"

"No, only for a few years. I guess from about ten until I went to high school. Everything changes in high school. I forgot about the dreams and never had them again. I mean, I still have dreams. But not like those. Those were something special."

"What were they about?"

"All sorts of things. My family a lot of the time. My friends. But mostly they were me in some exotic location doing something I could never really explain. I remember one. I was fighting a dragon that was attacking a village. I had armor and a horse and a heavy sword."

"You were never a princess, were you?" Debbie laughs.

"That's the funny thing, Deb. I was such a girly girl when I was awake. Not a tomboy at all. But never in those dreams. I was always active, and protecting or defending. I wasn't being saved or wishing some sweet prince would come along and sweep me off my feet. Well, not until later." Melissa laughs and then realizes it hurts to laugh and leans back with a heavy sigh. "I guess those dreams were just dreams. I wondered for a long time if they meant something."

"Maybe they do mean something, Liss."

"How, Deb? I can't even move my arm. I can't paint or sculpt anymore. My right arm. My brush hand. The hand that expressed my dreams."

Melissa Choi was one of the earliest participants with Nate and the others at the Columba. Indeed, her participation went beyond just the spiritual community when she took over as assistant manager. But before that she was an artist—an art-school graduate. A lot of her work filled the Columba pub. And in the last year her pieces started selling a lot more broadly after she had a particularly nice day at the PasadenART festival. She had quit her manager's job three months before as she found she didn't have even nearly enough time to devote to her passion, and finally she had the finances to begin to support her dream.

"But you're still alive. So there's always hope."

"Do you know what it feels like to lose something like that? To have everything collapse in an instant without it even being your fault?"

"Yes," Debbie replies. "I do."

"I'm sorry Deb, I didn't mean…."

"I know, Liss. I know."

"I guess I don't know what to do now. Those dreams. I don't know what to do with them now. The more I think about it the more I realize these dreams never left me, but have been in the back of my mind all my life, pushing me. Pushing me even stronger than my parents did. When my dreams clashed with my parents' dreams for me, that was the falling out."

"Have you talked to your dad yet? He keeps calling."

"I'm not ready. What do I say? I feel like he's going to be nice but underneath it all will be the message, 'I told you so.'"

"That you got shot? How do you see that?"

"If I had been a good wife and mother and followed what they had planned for me, then I would never have been in that neighborhood after an art show. Would have never been in that position. I left the plan, left the family. And see what happens? What did you do, Deb?"

"Do?"

"How did you find your way back?"

"When Courtney died?"

"Yeah. I don't know how to think. I don't know what I'm supposed to do."

"I just didn't know how to go on. Everyone sent me nice messages but I just knew they were only being nice and didn't really understand. Courtney was the only really nice thing that ever happened to me, Liss. So much darkness but my little girl was a light. A funny, loving, beacon of light. Every time I looked at her I knew God loved me too."

Debbie gets up and walks to the other side of the hospital bed and picks up the box of Kleenex. She stands a moment, staring out the window at the small lawn and much larger parking lot as she wipes her eyes.

"That's it for my mascara," she finally says, with a little attempt at a laugh.

"Deb, don't," Melissa says, leaning up again. "You don't have to."

"It's fine, Liss," Debbie replies. She walks back around the bed to the green cushioned chair and sits down. "I need to. For you and for me. What did I do, is that what you asked?"

"You don't have to say more," Melissa replies. "I'm sorry I asked. I wasn't thinking."

"For a while I didn't do anything. I just existed. I was totally empty. I stopped answering the door, stopped answering my phone."

"I remember that."

"Did I thank you for the food you left outside my door? I did appreciate it, and needed it."

"I know. We knew."

"I couldn't talk to anyone, not at all at first, and then not really for a long time after. I couldn't talk to God. What would I say? What would I say to him? He took away the love he had for me. It was too hard. Just when I was really getting close to God for the first time in my life—first real time—that car hit her. Just when I was feeling a sense of peace, Liss….Sorry."

Debbie takes another tissue and sits in silence for a moment. Melissa tries to lean over but a sharp pain hits her as she moves, so she leans back again, tears in her own eyes as well.

"Here," Debbie says, handing a few Kleenexes to Melissa.

when doubts and questions abound

"I had no place to go," Debbie continues. "I mean no place to go with my pain and hurt. I was so trapped. I still believed in God, Liss, but I didn't know who he was anymore—who he was to me. Why did he hate me? That was my prayer. 'Why do you hate me, God?' I sat on my couch, in the same clothes I had worn two days before to the funeral. And that was the only thing I could think. 'What did I do wrong to deserve this?' I started hearing all the cruel words from when I was growing up. Men who told me 'You deserve this' or 'You're a slut and should expect to be treated like one.' Men who said those things to me and abused me, then would stand up in church and give their testimonies like they somehow had special access to God. I believed them, Liss, even if part of me knew they were wrong. But after so much, I believed them in my heart. All that came back. That I didn't deserve anything. God had always hated me. Ever since I was born. You know what I did next?"

"What?"

"I didn't know where to start. So I just opened up my Bible. I opened it up to Psalm 88." She reaches over and opens a drawer in the dresser near the bed. Looks inside. Closes the drawer. Opens the second drawer. Looks inside.

"The Gideons haven't been by," Melissa says. "There's one in my bag right there."

"How did you know?" Debbie leans down and pulls out a Bible.

"It was either that or you were being rudely distracting."

"Ha." She flips a few pages. "Here it is: Psalm 88."

> ▶ O Lord, the God who saves me,
> day and night I cry out before you.
>
> May my prayer come before you;
> turn your ear to my cry.

How Long? 18

For my soul is full of trouble
and my life draws near the grave.

I am counted among those who go down to the pit;
I am like a man without strength.

I am set apart with the dead,
like the slain who lie in the grave,
whom you remember no more,
who are cut off from your care.

You have put me in the lowest pit,
in the darkest depths.

Your wrath lies heavily upon me;
you have overwhelmed me with all your waves.

You have taken from me my closest friends
and have made me repulsive to them.
I am confined and cannot escape;

my eyes are dim with grief.
I call to you, O Lord, every day;
I spread out my hands to you.

Do you show your wonders to the dead?
Do those who are dead rise up and praise you?

Is your love declared in the grave,
your faithfulness in Destruction?

Are your wonders known in the place of darkness,
or your righteous deeds in the land of oblivion?

But I cry to you for help, O Lord;
in the morning my prayer comes before you.

Why, O Lord, do you reject me
and hide your face from me?

From my youth I have been afflicted and close to death;
I have suffered your terrors and am in despair.

Your wrath has swept over me;
your terrors have destroyed me.

All day long they surround me like a flood;
they have completely engulfed me.

> You have taken my companions and loved ones from me;
> the darkness is my closest friend. Ω

"And that's how it ends, Liss. Just like that. I read this psalm and it said everything I was thinking, what I was feeling. It was so comforting; which is weird, I know. But it was. It made sense to me. All the nice words, the encouragements—the 'God is with you' statements—they were all so empty. Meaningless. But I opened my Bible and read this psalm and felt like I found real words. Words for me and from me."

"Well, they're so encouraging, Deb. Thanks for sharing them," Melissa laughs. "Nothing like wrath to cheer a person up."

"But that's it, Liss. I know, it's totally weird. There's no hope at all in this psalm, but that lack of hope makes so much sense to me. It's full of loss. Loss wallowed in and dwelled upon. No fruity words or religious sentiments. Pure sadness. That's where I was. Pure sadness, with no hope. I lost Courtney, my precious little girl. I couldn't even muster up fake hope. I didn't even want to believe. I got tired of hoping and trusting and waiting. I was finished. I had to mourn, mourn over Courtney, mourn what I lost and what I would never experience. Mourn all the evil of it. This psalm said that."

"That's kind of how I feel."

"No one ever showed me that psalm. It's like it never existed before. Have you heard it?"

"No," Melissa answers. "I once asked my dad why his sermons seemed to never touch on difficult stuff in the Bible. That was when I started to pull away and notice everything. He said that he only had forty minutes to encourage people in their faith and he didn't want to leave them with questions they couldn't answer. He didn't want to risk their stumbling or losing heart. They needed encouragement and trust, he said, not doubt. Doubt was Satan's job, not a pastor's."

"That sounds so right I guess, and I understand. But doubt came to me," Debbie says. "It not only came, it beat me up and left me on the side of the road for dead. I was robbed by life and that doubt—that giving up—was all I had. It screamed at me, and I had nothing to say to it; I'd never been given resources to cope. Except I had this psalm. It said what I needed to say. So I sat with it for a long time—for that whole afternoon. I got to wondering what else I should say. So I turned the pages back a little and spent some time with Psalm 77."

> ▶ I cried out to God for help;
> I cried out to God to hear me.
>
> When I was in distress, I sought the Lord;
> at night I stretched out untiring hands
> and my soul refused to be comforted.
>
> I remembered you, O God, and I groaned;
> I mused, and my spirit grew faint.
>
> You kept my eyes from closing;
> I was too troubled to speak.
>
> I thought about the former days,
> the years of long ago;
>
> I remembered my songs in the night.
> My heart mused and my spirit inquired:
>
> "Will the Lord reject forever?
> Will he never show his favor again?
>
> Has his unfailing love vanished forever?
> Has his promise failed for all time?
>
> Has God forgotten to be merciful?
> Has he in anger withheld his compassion?" Ω

"There it was," Debbie continues. "That's what I was feeling. Maybe he was angry. Maybe he had forgotten. His promise—Courtney—had vanished from my life. The promise failed. She was gone. Another psalm saying exactly what I didn't know how to say. I stopped in the middle of this psalm and just cried and cried and cried. All the stopped-up tears burst out. The dam broke. I didn't know I had that much water in me. For like an hour I just cried and cried. No thoughts. Nothing. Just tears. Then I picked up the Bible again and kept reading the rest of the psalm."

> ▶ Then I thought, "To this I will appeal:
> the years of the right hand of the Most High."
>
> I will remember the deeds of the Lord;
> yes, I will remember your miracles of long ago.
>
> I will meditate on all your works
> and consider all your mighty deeds.
>
> Your ways, O God, are holy.
> What god is so great as our God?
>
> You are the God who performs miracles;
> you display your power among the peoples.
>
> With your mighty arm you redeemed your people,
> the descendants of Jacob and Joseph.
>
> The waters saw you, O God,
> the waters saw you and writhed;
> the very depths were convulsed.
>
> The clouds poured down water,
> the skies resounded with thunder;
> your arrows flashed back and forth.
>
> Your thunder was heard in the whirlwind,
> your lightning lit up the world;
> the earth trembled and quaked.
>
> Your path led through the sea,
> your way through the mighty waters,
> though your footprints were not seen.
>
> You led your people like a flock
> by the hand of Moses and Aaron.   Ω

"I decided that I will remember," Debbie says. "I will meditate. I will consider—but not what's going on with me. I'll think about God. Look at what he has done. Remember the stories. The first part of the psalm was so true for me, Liss, that I thought maybe there was something to the second part too. I thought maybe it was telling me something."

"So you thought maybe there was some hope?"

"Yeah, and I read and read, kind of skimming over the stories in the Bible, starting from the beginning. The flood made so much sense to me, and I didn't really believe God when he said he wouldn't do that again. I felt like he had flooded me, because I was so wicked. I wasn't saved. I was outside the ark. But I kept reading and reading. Abraham and Isaac and Jacob. All of them. Then something stuck out so sharp. I started reading more closely."

"What was it?"

"The story of Joseph. God called him. Then everything in his life went downhill. He lost everything. All of who he was and wanted. That's how I felt too."

"I liked *Joseph and the Amazing Technicolor Dreamcoat*," Melissa says. She leans up a little and begins to sing, "I closed my eyes, drew back the curtain...."

Debbie joins in and they finish the verse together, "To see for certain what I thought I knew, Far far away, someone was weeping, But the world was sleeping, Any dream will do."

They stop as Melissa begins to cough. She winces in pain, and tries to drink some water. Debbie holds the cup for her, until she's had a long drink.

"...A crash of drums," Debbie continues to sing, standing and walking to the window as she continues. "A flash of light, My golden coat flew out of sight, The colors faded into darkness, I was left alone." After staring out the window a moment she repeats without singing, "I was left alone."

"You weren't really alone, Deb," Melissa says.

"I know; I know you were all around," she replies, looking back at Melissa. "But with Courtney gone and God so gone, too, I felt deeply alone. More alone than ever. Spiritually alone. But that's maybe what I saw in Joseph." Debbie walks back around to the other side of the bed and sits in the barely cushioned chair. "I got to wondering how Joseph felt in the middle of the story. When he was sitting in prison even though he didn't have sex with Potiphar's slut wife. That's what really got me. And it got me thinking. Thinking a lot. When I sort of figured it out, it didn't give me back Courtney or take away the pain, but it kind of made sense."

"What?"

"My feelings of loss and pain. I always thought pain was a sign God was gone. Only that's not true. Where was he when Joseph was in prison, Liss?"

"I don't know."

"Know what I think?"

"What?"

"I think he was with him. I think God was in the prison with him."

"What do you mean?"

"I don't really know, Liss. But it gives me goose bumps. God was in the prison with Joseph. He was watching Joseph when he ran away from Potiphar's slut wife and then when Joseph was being accused. God was standing by him."

"Like when Jesus was on trial before Pilate."

"Yes! That's what I mean. He was there with Joseph too. Standing with him, and when Joseph got sent to prison, God hadn't rejected him; he went with him into prison too. With him. Not against him. Whatever our prison is, God goes into prison with us. All my life I was told God is too big. Too holy. Too whatever. Anything negative is a sign of his absence. But there he was in prison, with Joseph."

"What's the psalm that Karl talked about a few weeks ago? The one that mentions Joseph?"

"Oh yeah! I was going to mention that to you. I wrote that down in my little notebook. Here. Psalm 105."

> ▶ He called down famine on the land
> and destroyed all their supplies of food;
>
> and he sent a man before them—
> Joseph, sold as a slave.
>
> They bruised his feet with shackles,
> his neck was put in irons,
>
> till what he foretold came to pass,
> till the word of the Lord proved him true.
> *(Psalm 105:16-19)* Ω

"I even wrote down what he said about it," Debbie continues. "He said that the Hebrew—I had no idea how to spell what he said—meant something different. It's not necessarily his neck in irons; it might be better put that the iron entered his soul. That's so it, isn't it? The irons, the chains, the prison—all of it actually got into his very soul."

"Just like my IV. Reminds me and traps me. At least that's how I feel. Shoved into the arm that I can't use anymore."

"You always go the extra mile for your performance pieces, Liss," Deb says, trying to get Melissa to laugh a little. It works.

"Don't make me laugh," Melissa says. "It hurts."

"I'll stop," Debbie replies. "No more jokes. Back to being serious."

"For now, at least," Melissa replies, adding a smile.

"For as long as I can manage," Debbie says.

"I guess," Debbie continues, "I saw people in the Bible as these real heroes—so much larger than me or anyone I knew. Not even real people. They were all characters. They were like these models created to make us work harder and do more and feel bad about our own lives. But that's not true at all. That psalm says Joseph wasn't happy and carefree no matter where he was. He felt it all. It weighed on him. And realizing that made everything different for me."

"Why?"

"Why? I don't know really," Debbie laughs. "Seems strange. I guess it was because all the nice Christian words, all the typical Christian messages made me feel like I had to somehow think it was okay that Courtney died, that I had to forget it or excuse it or feel spiritual about it. They made me feel like I had to answer those terrible, terrible questions in my heart with cutesy religious answers. I just couldn't do that and I couldn't stand hearing any more of that crap."

"People don't know what to say. And they don't like there not being an answer."

"That's what it is; but sometimes there isn't an answer," Debbie says.

"Which is too depressing. We don't know what to believe. So what do we believe?"

"Evil happens. It's not God who makes the evil happen. It's not God who asks for us to accept the evil that happens, calling it some crappy version of good. I realized I didn't have to accept that Courtney's death was somehow part of God's divine plan. I realized I didn't have to somehow see it as better that she's not with me, alive and laughing, going to school and coming home and meeting boys and all the things she should have experienced. That's not the point. The point is that Joseph being in prison—all the crap that happened to him—wasn't a sign of God's disfavor. God didn't abandon him. God went with him. Where was God when Joseph was in prison? Right there. Right there. Where was God when I was sitting in my apartment totally overwhelmed? He was with me. He was mourning with me. He wept too, Liss. Jesus was weeping too. With me, not against me."

"This is going to sound terrible, Deb. Don't hate me. But why does that help? How did it help you to think that God was with you after Courtney died? Where was he to stop Courtney from dying? I don't care that God is with me now. I can't sculpt! I can't paint anymore! I can't do anything. All that I was sure he asked me to do—I can't do it now. He makes demands and then he takes away all the ability to fulfill them. He robs me and then I am supposed to want him next to me? I'm mad at him, Deb! I'm pissed off and I don't know what to do about it." She stops as the tears take over. Deb hands her some tissues. "I'm sorry, Deb. I'm sorry. It just broke out. I've been keeping that in."

"Don't you think I said those things too? I've had time now, so I probably make it sound so…so rational and easy and everything. The reason it helps, Liss…well, I had to first see that God wasn't against me. And God isn't against you. Just because this happened doesn't mean that somehow God has rejected you. I know, I know. That sounds so trite. But it's true. Joseph was in prison. Sold as a slave. It wasn't right or good or somehow okay. But God was with him throughout all of it. And not only that, God used it. God used it."

"So he made all that happen so something good will come out of it? How does that make God seem better?"

"No. That's not what I'm saying. It happened; God used it. God was with Joseph throughout all of it. God was with Joseph in the dry well, and God was sold into slavery when Joseph was. God was with Joseph as he worked for Potiphar and God was with Joseph when he was tossed into jail. And all this isn't saying those were good things. It's saying that those *weren't* hopeless. Everything got stolen from Joseph, but with God there, Joseph still had hope. Courtney was stolen from me, Liss. Stolen. Stolen by a stupid man who couldn't just stop with one beer. Stolen. And I don't have to say that's okay. But I also don't have to think that everything is gone—that my life is hopeless and there's nothing left for me. I don't have to see it like that. The Bible doesn't tell me that all of that is okay. It says there is sin and evil in this world—sin and evil that God hates even more than I do. The Bible doesn't tell me that I have to be perfect and live a perfect life and have only pretty, lovely things happen to me. The Scriptures don't tell me that the sign of God's presence is constant happiness, and riches, and all that I could possibly want."

"They tell you about Joseph."

"They tell me about Joseph and everyone else. They tell me about the cross, Liss. I saw this and realized all those pretty, heroic characters in the Bible—all those I thought were these models of perfection—had crap hit them from every direction. So why don't we expect it then? Why haven't we been taught that crappy lives aren't a sign of God's disfavor? Life happens and the Bible is filled, *filled*, with all kinds of life—a lot of it worse than what has happened to us. That's not the point. The stuff isn't the point; that's what I saw. The point is that God is with us, and that only by staying with him—even with all of that crap happening around us—we will see freedom and hope and life. God doesn't make us think that bad is good, and that crap is chocolate cake. 'Just eat it and you'll like it.' No. God says that this stuff, all of it, is what happens and we're not asked to justify it or justify God or ourselves or anything. He tells us—tells us all through Scripture—that he'll stick with us and that we need to stick with him, because what we see isn't the end of the story. It's not over. There's more, and the only hope we can possibly have is to have faith that he's playing to win. Playing to win everything. But that doesn't mean in the middle there won't be disasters and problems and all the crap that happens."

"So we're supposed to have faith, no matter what?"

"That's it, Liss," Debbie says. "That's what I'm saying. Look at those stories. There are some miracles, sure. But a lot of hurt and heartache and confusion and frustration. What happened to us isn't some kind of rejection or sign that God hates us. We're part of this chapter, you see. That's what I saw. I was with Joseph in prison too. And I stopped waiting for God to say how lovely prison is or that I should be happy with it. No! I started waiting to be let out of prison with Joseph. To be, like the Israelites, set free from Egypt. 'Let my people go,' right? That's faith. And that's hope. That's how I can live. That's how I started piecing my life back together—with the faith talked about here. Not the flimsy, silly, everything-is-okay kind of faith. In the face of all the crap, faith is realizing God is still with me and realizing he plays to win. Right now we're neither here nor there. But we have to expect there is a 'there.' Something more than all of this. That's the kind of faith that keeps me moving still."

"I don't know if I can have that kind of faith, Deb," Melissa says, tears in her eyes. "I don't know how. I can't. I don't see it. I don't understand. I don't have faith and I don't know how to."

"I know," Debbie says. She stands up and leans over the bed, hugs Melissa. "I know."

If you have any encouragement from being united with Christ, if any comfort from his love, if any fellowship with the Spirit, if any tenderness and compassion, then make my joy complete by being like-minded, having the same love, being one in spirit and purpose.

(Philippians 2:1-2)

4

when that unsettled feeling hangs on

The second floor of the Columba contains a large room, accessible by stairs or by a small elevator. Formerly the room was used for banquets or other large group parties, but when Nate and the others took over running the Columba they realized the space could have a much more important purpose. Nate and his friends took out the large tables and most of the chairs, and replaced them with couches, smaller tables, and a wide assortment of decorations. The décor became a mix of reproductions of historical Christian art from a wide variety of traditions, and unique contributions made by those who find regular spiritual community at the Columba. The room is a meeting place for the gathered community; on Sunday evenings people meet for what some might call their weekly service. But this room is also a place to pray, to read, to cry, to share. It is not, Nate would argue, the place where the ministry takes place. Ministry takes place wherever the Spirit calls them to be—downstairs in the pub, or out and about. Wherever they can help shine light and exhibit what it means to be part of the people of God in this world.

For people stretched thin, this room is an oasis of renewal and restoration, quiet and focus, and rejuvenation for ministry. It is a place of worship, a place encouraging contemplation in the midst of a busy city. This room is known, not surprisingly, as the Upper Room. People who gather regularly and are committed to each other, to the mission of the Columba, and to seeing a renewed work of the Spirit blossom in this neighborhood tend to informally refer to themselves as part of the Upper Room community.

Because Nate and the others see this room as an oasis and as a gift for the community, the Upper Room is accessible almost anytime the Columba is open. And three times a day, people use the room as a place for communal prayer: in the morning at around seven, at noon, and in the evening at around seven. Usually, this prayer time lasts about twenty minutes, and consists of liturgical prayers and the spontaneous prayers of those who feel words of God rising out of their souls.

On this particular Thursday, Nate lingers upstairs after the prayer time, still feeling spiritual parched, out of tune, off the path, or whatever other analogy can describe a temporarily troubled theology. Mike Kivitz is also lingering, staying after everyone except for Nate has gone. At first Mike feels stirred to pray for his kids—his own kids and his high school students. But, for some reason, he can't focus on his kids and instead keeps wondering about Nate. Rather than fighting the distraction, Mike gets up off the lounge chair and walks to the other side of the room.

"Can I pray for you?" he asks Nate, who is hunched over in his chair, his elbows on his knees, his hands over his eyes.

Nate looks up. He is about to respond with the typical, "no thanks, I'm fine" but then realizes he's not fine.

"Do you have time to talk?" Nate asks.

"Just so happens I have fifth period free," Mike responds, "But I do have to get back for sixth period, so that gives us an hour. That enough time?"

"For now," Nate laughs.

"What's up?" Mike asks. The floodgates open. While Nate is a bit surprised by how much he has to say once given the chance, Mike isn't.

Mike Kivitz is the oldest of those committed to the spiritual community at the Columba. His once dark brown hair is now more than half gray, and more than half gone. "Well-lived-in" he says of himself, and tends to add "slightly paunchy" to his description. Mike served as an influential pastor at a megachurch in the Midwest for a number of years before stepping away after a scandal—he had an affair with a younger woman who proclaimed all kinds of other charges. While most of the charges were untrue, they were believable. His marriage fell apart and he hasn't returned to full-time ministry since. When he and his second wife, Rachel, joined the community at the Columba four years ago, he felt tempted at first to look for a leadership role and push himself forward. But he backed away from those pursuits, helped by those around him. He has since found contentment as an English teacher and as the occasional humbled conversation partner with struggling ministry leaders.

After about twenty minutes of Nate talking and Mike mostly just nodding or adding the occasional "go on" or "I totally understand," Nate finally realizes he is beginning to repeat the same frustrations again and again, merely putting them in different words to better help describe what he can't quite figure out.

"Do you think I'm just whining?" Nate asks.

"Well, yeah," Mike laughs. "But that's not the point, is it?"

"Thanks....So what is the point?"

"Is your whining about something real? I mean are you just trying to find something to whine about or is it an understandable struggle? Are you wallowing in your whining or are you interested in it bringing you somewhere?"

"Wallowing in whining. That would make a good name for a band."

"Or an art film," Mike replies. "In fact, I think Rachel took me to see that at the Laemmle Theatre last month."

"Do *you* think I'm whining about something real?"

"Of course you are. I mean, look what has happened, Nate. Melissa is in the hospital, your car was stolen, that article—that you thought would broaden your influence and be a great step in your ministry—was lost and it's gone too far past the deadline. And all the other stuff. Put those together and it's something."

"What do you mean, 'other stuff'? Life was good. Until Thursday."

"Nate, who are you talking to? Life is good on the outside and that masks what's inside. You can't sit there and tell me that with all that has happened recently you're not thinking about all that has happened to you in the past."

"What happened in the past?"

"Nate, your fiancée left you! Your church didn't have room for you! You're living in a small apartment over a busy pub! You're not famous!"

"I'll give you the first ones, even if I don't think those bother me anymore. But not that last one. I don't care about being famous."

"Nate, of course you do. You want to matter. Not just for us here; you want to change the church. Everywhere. You want to let people know what's going on. You want to have a voice. You're a prophet, Nate, and have had a limited audience. I know what that's like. You feel that drive. That discontent. Especially now."

"Why especially now? And I don't think wanting to have a voice is the same thing as wanting to be famous."

"You're on your sixth year here. Things are moving along. Everything is good. You leave for a few weeks and we keep on going. We don't need you."

"Thanks," Nate laughs.

"You know what I mean. You're a builder, a shaper, a changer. You've set that up and things are rolling along nicely. Small challenges pop up but you've basically worked yourself out of a job and now you're ready to step up to a new level."

"I should start a new church?"

"Ha! Now that's what I'm talking about."

"I should then?"

"I don't know. I mean, you're exposing yourself here. You asked that question. That huge question. I doubt you've ever even said that out loud to yourself. But that question has been there in your mind, and when I say 'step up to a new level' that's the direction you jump at."

Nate doesn't say anything.

"You're not me," Mike says. "Thank God for that. We don't need another me. But, to be honest, I don't think you're you either. You're trying to find that thing—that thing that will give you the next step. Fulfillment."

"Which only comes through my identity with Christ."

"Absolutely. Absolutely, Nate. You know that. I know that. But maybe you only know that in your head. You know the right words. What, really, is your identity with Christ?"

"Everything. I gave up everything, Mike. Let it all go. I'm here doing what I'm supposed to do. Living my life as a missionary. Trying to tap into the work of the Spirit in my life and in the lives of everyone I meet. I'm doing, you know. I'm participating. I'm helping and giving. I'm seeking Jesus in every part of my life."

"And?"

"And so why am I so knocked off track with all this stuff that's happening? My car is just a car. There's a lot up in the air with Melissa still, but she's alive and recovering. The article? That's just one of those things, and maybe it'll still work out for another issue. It all hit me hard, sure. But it's lingering. That's what I don't get. It's not that big of a deal."

"Only it is."

"Yeah. Only it is."

"Huge. Everything," Mike says.

"What else do I have? Who am I now? For the future? What I don't get, Mike, is that I know those answers. I mean, if a reporter came up to me and asked, I could talk for hours about the work of God and the attitudes we are supposed to have, the things we should do, all those ways we participate with the Spirit. I've given those answers. Still could. With total sincerity."

"And you do that really well. Better than I ever did. You know the heart of God, Nate. You know and seek Christ. You do participate with the Spirit."

"So what am I doing wrong?"

Mike laughs. "Why do you think you're doing something wrong?"

"I'm still confused. I don't even know how to talk about that confusion. I'm not hiding anything, I just don't know what to say to anyone. To myself."

"What is God saying?"

Nate pauses.

"Nothing. Maybe that's it. Maybe that's most of it, Mike. I'm not hearing from God. I pray and nothing. Nothing. Which means something, you know. Only I don't know what, because I don't know what I'm doing wrong."

"So you want to know how to fix it? You want to know what you're doing wrong? How to get yourself back to feeling like you did when you left your church and got offered a restaurant and a new community? You want to pray and see Jesus again, like you did before, like when you felt pushed to do something new. You want that back."

"That's what I want."

"Can I be honest?"

"Absolutely."

"I think you're supposed to stay. I think you're supposed to rediscover your vision within this place. I think you are supposed to find a depth of God that you haven't found before. I think you're not at the end of your race. You have no idea what it is that's still ahead, but God does."

"So what do I do then? Honestly, Mike, it would feel really good to get up right now, pack up my things, and move somewhere totally different. Get a fresh start again. Feel the thrill of a whole new reality. I've got that apostolic burn."

"But is it a Spirit burn? That's the question. You're faced with this almost overwhelming urge to step up. But what does that mean? Is starting something new the only expression of that?"

"It's the only thing that comes to mind."

"But that's because it's the only thing you know. It's the only way you've experienced change. You change settings. Settings change around you. You feel this burn and you think this has to mean a change of location or people or whatever. Is that the Spirit, Nate? Or is that you taking your present understanding and applying it to this new situation?"

"Maybe it is the Spirit working in what I know."

"Maybe it is. Or maybe it's the Spirit leading you to a new lesson, but if you take the response of old lessons, you'll go back into a loop, forever repeating the same experience."

"So what, then?"

"You must have the same attitude that Christ Jesus had."

"Right. Which means what?"

"Philippians 2, Nate. Come on! And you, a pastor," Mike laughs. "We even talked about this a while back."

> ▶ If you have any encouragement from being united with Christ, if any comfort from his love, if any fellowship with the Spirit, if any tenderness and compassion, then make my joy complete by being like-minded, having the same love, being one in spirit and purpose. Do nothing out of selfish ambition or vain conceit, but in humility consider others better than yourselves. Each of you should look not only to your own interests, but also to the interests of others.
>
> Your attitude should be the same as that of Christ Jesus:
>
> Who, being in very nature God, did not consider equality with God something to be grasped, but made himself nothing, taking the very nature of a servant, being made in human likeness. And being found in appearance as a man, he humbled himself and became obedient to death—even death on a cross! Therefore God exalted him to the highest place and gave him the name that is above every name, that at the name of Jesus every knee should bow, in heaven and on earth and under the earth, and

> every tongue confess that Jesus Christ is Lord,
> to the glory of God the Father.
>
> Therefore, my dear friends, as you have always
> obeyed—not only in my presence, but now
> much more in my absence—continue to work
> out your salvation with fear and trembling, for
> it is God who works in you to will and to act
> according to his good purpose.
>
> Do everything without complaining or arguing,
> so that you may become blameless and pure,
> children of God without fault in a crooked and
> depraved generation, in which you shine like
> stars in the universe. (Philippians 2:1-15)   Ω

"This is the example of Christ, Nate. This is also the *identity* of Christ. That was the lesson God taught me, is still teaching me. I tried to be God's representative on earth by being someone special, by being someone in charge, by being someone who served others by getting them to serve me. I had to let go of the identity I had. We look to the moment, to this present, to the story that we know so far. We forget the rest. I think that's one of the biggest failings of a lot of Christians I've met. They think the mission of God is for the here and now."

"But it is! The good news is for the here and now."

"It is. But it isn't *just* for the here and now. That's the problem, you see. The Spirit, who is the living mission of God with us, leads us toward doing and being in this moment. Only, the good news is also about bringing us to a place where we are in full relationship with God. We're not going around in a circle. He's taking us somewhere."

"Is he taking us to his identity? We become broken to become like Jesus?"

"That's it," Mike says. "But we're all at different places in that process, you know. Some of us, like me, need to be broken.

Some need to be lifted up because they're already broken. Some are blind to their own brokenness and are surprised when they are confronted with it. That's precisely when we see how much we need Christ's work. We have to let go of it all—one way or another—to be able to really let Christ shape us into who we are supposed to be."

"The suffering isn't the point, but it might be part of the path. It's part of the rhythm of our spiritual lives. Right?"

"Exactly! That's why I say my suffering was from God, and I try to do my absolute most to help others in their suffering, so that they can see God."

"I need to stop focusing on the particulars and see how what I'm dealing with is steering me toward my identity in Christ, to become like Jesus," Nate says.

"That's exactly why I'm thinking you're not supposed to leave. What does leaving do? It folds you back into your most comfortable situation where once again you can lead and shape while bringing others to their role. You replay the last couple of years in a new setting. Sure, there are a few differences. Sure, you've learned lessons. But it's a replaying."

"Are you sure I'm not supposed to start a new church?"

"Am I the Holy Spirit?"

"Hmmm, you're not fiery enough, I think," Nate laughs.

"I don't know, Nate. Maybe you are. Supposed to start a new church, I mean." Mike smiles for a moment and then quickly becomes serious again. "But it seems to me, with all that I know, that you're hitting a wall. Only it's not a wall of what you're supposed to do, but a wall of who you are supposed to be. That's God's mission, you see. That's what he's about. He's drawing everyone to him and into him, so that we all take on our right identity in and with Christ. God moves. He frustrates.

He enlightens. He brings us through dark nights and bright days."

"So, I'm in a wilderness. And that's a good thing?"

"I guess so," Mike laughs. "Though sometimes I wish we'd get a syllabus early in the process rather than afterward."

"That would take away all the fun," Nate laughs.

Mike is silent for a moment, then says, "You know, Nate, the more I think about it, the more I think you do need to go."

"Really?" Nate looks a little shocked.

"For a while at least. The more I think about it, the more I think you're probably spinning in circles. I know the feeling, and it took getting me away from myself for a while."

"Where would that be? I always seem to be around wherever I go," Nate laughs.

"I've got this friend. He was a real mentor to me when I was in college. A professor then. He moved out to California when I was just starting out in ministry, to start a church. I lost touch with him for a long while until I got a really frustrating note from him."

"You're a great salesman, Mike."

"Yeah, well, it was really frustrating because his note came right when I was at the peak of my church-and-politics life. Right when everything seemed together. He told me I was off track and I was going to find correction if I wasn't careful. Something like that at least. I ignored the note, ended up getting into trouble, and God corrected me. So he was exactly right, which added to the frustration. He was the reason I decided to come to California when I had to get away from Ohio. You should talk to him. I think it would be helpful."

"Where's he now?"

"Big Bear, in the mountains. He's retired now from full-time ministry. Lives up where he can listen to the birds and wind, he says."

"That's a couple hours away. Maybe when things clear up around here, I'll go."

"No, Nate, I think you should go now. Stay a while, if he's open to it, and I'll bet he will be. Go while things still aren't clear. While everything is unsettled."

"Mike, I'm needed here. For Melissa. With everything that's going on, I can't just go out there now."

"That's exactly why I think you should go now. You think you're needed. You're not. Especially now. You think it's up to you and it's all your responsibility. You think you have a power. Let it go, Nate. Let it go. We like you, but we don't need you here."

"I'll think about it."

"You do that. His name is Joseph. I'll give you his number."

"God is about relationship. He wants the whole world to be in relationship with him. He wants each of us to be in a real relationship with him throughout eternity. And that's a process. We all participate in ways: outreach, evangelism, service, reaching out. But if we're not getting ourselves and others into a real relationship with God, it's all a waste."

5

when 'being' trumps 'doing'

"So they sent you away, did they?" Joseph says as he fills Nate's cup a second time. "Good people. Know enough to know enough."

"I'm a little offended, really," Nate laughs. "Not a single one of them said I should stay. I was hoping for a little support, Joseph."

"Support for what? And, again, call me Joe."

"Alright, Joe. Support for staying, sticking around, doing what I do best."

"What is it you do best?" Joseph runs his hand through his wispy white hair. He seems to have avoided baldness for as long as possible, his hair merely thinning all over without making too much fuss about it. He never was a tall man, a little below average height, with increasing arthritis now taking even more from him. He wears a red flannel shirt—one of five shirts he rotates through during the week—and his ten-year-old, faded Levi's 501 jeans.

"I listen," Nate answers. "And I talk. I don't know....I think God's used me to pass on wisdom and direction, maybe show people how to see the Spirit in their lives."

"Sounds to me like you've gotten to the end of what you know."

"What do you mean?"

"Would they have sent you away if you were really able to tell them something they didn't know, something they hadn't heard from you before or from each other?"

"That's my problem, then. I guess I don't feel like I have anywhere else to lead these people. That's why I'm thinking about a new place, where I could start fresh again, and maybe help bring a spark to some more folks."

"Then when you've done that?"

"Try it again."

"Like Paul."

"Exactly, Joe. Like Paul."

"Are you Paul?"

"I suppose I am. Or I should be."

"Maybe you should be, maybe you shouldn't. Have you ever been knocked to the ground and blinded?"

"Not literally."

"Have you ever persecuted Christians because of your zealousness for the law that you thought was God's?"

"Not intentionally."

"Maybe then you have a different story than Paul. A different role. A different path."

"I've no desire to go to Asia Minor," Nate says.

"Now see," Joseph laughs, "you're getting it. Tell me, Nate, about your call. When did you first feel God was calling you?"

"To the Upper Room? To ministry? To what?"

"Calling you, Nate. When did you first feel this pull to God, like he had called out your name and was telling you he wanted you? Something like that ever happen?"

"Yeah. When I was about ten or so."

"What was it like?"

"I remember I was sitting in my room. It was late at night, I should have been asleep. I felt—I still remember this so strongly—absolutely certain God existed. I had gone to church all my life but it was just part of life. That was the moment God introduced himself. I felt like I had meaning. I remember the next day casually telling my mom that I was going to be a pastor. She asked why I would say that. 'I don't know,' I replied. 'I just feel like it.' I haven't thought about that in a long time, but I guess that's when I first felt God calling me."

"To ministry?"

"No. But that was my response to it, I think. God wasn't that specific. I just felt…important, meaningful."

"Were you flooded with angst in the months before? Did you have long talks with your parents? What did you do leading up to that moment in your bedroom?"

"Nothing. It was totally unexpected. I wouldn't have even known to look for something like that."

"So why now? You think God gave you that moment just for a little thrill?"

"No."

"I don't mean to be cranky with you, Nate. It's just that I'm seventy-eight years old and I've been around this world for a long time, and have a good knowledge of people who were around for a long time themselves. So I've seen and heard a few things."

"That's why I'm here, Joe. I need to listen a while, I suppose."

"That's what Mike told you, right?" Joseph laughs. "You don't believe it quite yet."

"I'm thinking he had a point."

"You young leaders haven't changed. I remember just starting out and the world was up to me. God had called me and I better do something about it. And you know what?"

"What?"

"I did. I got into the game and did my part. I led churches and preached the gospel. I helped train new young leaders. I left that to start all over again and do church planting. I was Pastor Joseph Gariante, full of dreams and hopes and truth—and words, lots of words. I was commissioned for the Great Commission and I wanted to see the whole world evangelized in my generation. I couldn't do it alone, but with like-minded others and the power of the Holy Spirit it was possible. God had given us a chance and a mission. You understand what I'm saying don't you, Nate?"

"Yeah."

"I kept focused. I kept my heart pure and my mind on Christ. I didn't stray. I didn't have some kind of major fall like so many around me did. So many fell like flies. Sex. Money. All sorts of reasons—all based on pride and power and losing focus on Christ our Savior. I pressed on, Nate, I pressed on. Kept my focus where I thought it should be. Fought the good fight, and kept fighting. God's work was accomplished. It certainly was. But that work, it wasn't enough. When troubles came, when they finally came, I had nothing deep. Nothing that was mine. It was all for other people. I had words for them. Good words, Nate, good words. But they kept me busy and away from myself. Now, why am I telling you all this?"

"I don't know."

"Because I want you to know my story, so that you don't make assumptions about who I am or what I've done. What makes a man leave a church and go to the mountains? You asked yourself that on the way here, didn't you? You know Mike's story. You know how he fell from grace, like so many of my friends and students and fellow laborers did. It's the big wall—sin. God doesn't let you get away with it for too long. But I don't have that in my story. I didn't come here to retire, Nate. I came because I was fed up with God. That's right, fed up. I hadn't done a thing wrong. I'd done so much right and then when I was expecting to settle down a little bit and maybe write or garden or read I didn't get my supposed promised land. Instead I got emptiness and desert. You're not married are you?"

"Was going to be. She left me not long before the wedding."

"She left you before you got married. Well, imagine if she had left you forty years after you got married, Nate, and it wasn't even her choice. My Maggie got breast cancer eighteen years ago and that was that. It took over. In eight months we went from perfect bliss to me praying with her on her deathbed. God's will, people told me. Damn you, I responded. Pardon my language."

"It's alright."

"I'm not asking for *your* pardon, Nate. I did everything right, you hear me? Still, I lost it all. How many funerals had I preached at? A lot. I said all the right words, had all the right verses. Sometimes they made sense, sometimes they didn't. But I always had something appropriate and helpful to say. When it happened to me, well, that was it. I figured I had done enough for God and I would just go ahead and live my life the way I wanted. Move away from people. Move away from my past. Just finish out my days. You want some more coffee?"

"That'd be great. But I'll get it." Nate gets up and walks into the kitchen.

"Cream is on the second shelf in the fridge," Joseph says, raising his voice so Nate can hear. "Can you bring me a glass of water? Glasses are in the cabinet next to the sink. I'm not used to talking this much and figure I've got a lot more to say."

"Oh, thank you," Joseph says, as Nate hands him a glass of water.

Nate sits down and takes a sip of the hot, dark coffee. He hasn't been sleeping well, and the long drive made him a little more drowsy than he expected. Or maybe it was the forest air. Or something else.

"Thing is, Nate, that I thought God had called me to do something back when I was young and excitable. But God hadn't called me to *do*," Joseph says. "He just called me. You see the distinction?"

"He wanted you, not what you could do for him."

"That's right. Only we want to give and those of us who give so much forget there is anything besides the giving, and never get around to realizing what God is about. It's only when I stopped talking that I started to listen, and God started telling me all kinds of things."

"Such as?"

"Such as Abraham," Joseph says. "Such as all kinds of stories in the Old Testament. And the New, for that matter. What does it mean when God calls?"

"Mission." Nate replies. "When I prayed for God to work, for the Spirit to work, doors began to open up and we stepped into a new way of doing things. We started the Columba, and the Upper Room. Called from the bondage we felt before, to a new freedom—embracing the promise."

"So now that you're in your supposed promised land and things are going wrong," Joseph says, "you figure you better start reading the Prophets to see what you're doing wrong—why God's judgment is coming down upon you? Maybe you're not hearing right. Or someone is holding on to something they shouldn't. Or maybe you've ignored God's push in your life in some way. Missed out on the chance to do right and good. Made a mistake in listening, did you?"

"Maybe. I feel dry. The words that used to help seem artificial now. Which makes me think I'm losing my faith, losing something, and I need to get a charge in a new place to find it again."

"So that's it. You're worried you're losing your faith because you feel dry within the challenges? So you want to do something that might reignite it. Find what it is that seems to be the answer and somehow get yourself back on the track. Start running again, really running. Not slogging day after day like you are now."

"Yes. That's it," Nate responds. "I guess."

"Works."

"What?"

"Works. As much as you deny it, Nate, you think God is about works. You want to see and feel and do. You want to perform. And if you're not getting the applause you think there's something wrong with the performance. You don't think God will show up when he wants you. You think you have to keep bringing to him. You forget what happened when you were ten and you had absolutely no expectations. You think that the dryness or the emptiness or the frustration or the loss or whatever is some kind of divine sign. You're going by cues, cues that you design. Works."

"You brought up Abraham, Joe. Abraham was called, and called to go, to do."

"Go where? Do what? Hand me the Bible that's on that table there, by the window." Nate gets up and walks over to the window, looking outside as he does so. Two jays, perched in the cedar tree outside, each on a different branch, look right at him. One begins to squawk rather raucously. Nate picks up the Bible and looks back at Joseph with a bit of alarm.

"Oh, don't mind them. They just want some peanuts," Joseph says, and then turns and looks out the window. "I'm out of peanuts," he yells. "More tomorrow." The birds hop to different branches and after one last look fly away. Nate swears they knew exactly what Joe meant. He walks back across the room and hands Joseph the Bible.

"Here it is," Joseph says, after turning a few pages. "Listen closely."

> ▶ The Lord had said to Abram, "Leave your country, your people and your father's household and go to the land I will show you.
>
> "I will make you into a great nation
> and I will bless you;
> I will make your name great,
> and you will be a blessing.
>
> I will bless those who bless you,
> and whoever curses you I will curse;
> and all peoples on earth
> will be blessed through you."
>
> So Abram left, as the Lord had told him; and Lot went with him. Abram was seventy-five

> years old when he set out from Haran. He took
> his wife Sarai, his nephew Lot, all the posses-
> sions they had accumulated and the people
> they had acquired in Haran, and they set out
> for the land of Canaan, and they arrived there.
>
> Abram traveled through the land as far as the
> site of the great tree of Moreh at Shechem.
> At that time the Canaanites were in the land.
> The Lord appeared to Abram and said,
> "To your offspring I will give this land."
> So he built an altar there to the Lord,
> who had appeared to him.
> *(Genesis 12:1-7)* Ω

"So, God called Abraham to go. To go where?" Joseph asks again.

"To the land God will show him," Nate answers.

"More than that. Read what comes after. Go to the land, sure, but then it's 'I will make,' 'I will bless,' 'I will give.' All Abraham had to do was listen and go to the land God showed him. But what you're talking about is looking and searching, trying to figure out and work, make things happen. Go where you want and expect God to follow along, applauding when you do a neat new trick. You're tired of listening. You're tired of the dryness. You've never been at this point before. There was always some new program or new group of people or new whatever to start and do. You see it in ministry, but it's true for every area. People feel like this with work, or friendships, or marriages. How many marriages collapse because people feel bored and think they've come to an end? So the man and woman just find another person to get emotional with, calling that shallow emotion 'love' and upsetting lives. Do you support that kind of thing?"

"No."

"Why?"

"Because I've heard from people who have been married a while that there is something more if they stick it out. And we're called to be committed in marriage."

"So that's that. There's more. But we—and I'm talking about myself here, too—don't teach about the *more* that is available. We say go out and do, and if you're feeling dry you're not doing enough, not offering enough. There's never an end, and we blame people, blame ourselves, Nate, for not doing enough. Maggie died and I blamed myself. God was punishing me for not doing enough. I wracked my brain to figure out what it was and came up with all kinds of answers. Things I did that year, things I had not done thirty years before. I knew in my head I was wrong to think like this, but my heart didn't care. That was the answer that made sense. I had to blame, and it was better for me to blame myself than to blame God. What would I do if I started blaming God?"

"You'd lose your hope."

"Oh, that's the nice pastor thing to say, isn't it? Lose my hope. What hope did I have if God had already rejected me? That's what I felt. Maggie wasn't just my wife, Nate. She was my best friend, my coworker, my foundation. She was everything to me. And then I got to thinking maybe she was an idol of sorts, and God was teaching me. But I couldn't accept that. What kind of loving God would use that lesson, Nate? No definition of love I could come up with would justify that. What could I preach after that, asking those kinds of questions? What could I tell people? I had all the answers and then none of them were suitable anymore."

"So you left your church and went elsewhere?"

"Darn right I did. I left my church. Came up here. God was done with me, I was done with God. That's what I thought. But God has a way—ha!—God has a way. He calls and doesn't let a person forget it. I learned a few things and then a few things more and got to really reading all over again. I had to know who this God was. How he worked."

"What did you find?"

"That everything I had been told was wrong."

"I know that feeling," Nate laughs.

"It is unsettling, because when you see it you realize how obvious it is, and you think someone should have told you years before so you could really learn how life works. Then you look back and wonder how knowing would have changed conversations, or actions, or ministry goals. How much more effective would I have been?"

"What was it you learned?"

"Look at Abraham, Nate! Look at his life. You see the promise and jump right to the end. I hear about call and I think that's the way. Just do and go. Just do and go. Everything works out. The promised land. And if it doesn't work out then what do we do? We skip to the prophets and all their messages of woe caused by the Israelites turning away from God. What about the middle? The middle of what happened with Abraham; the middle of all the stories. I thought about that and I realized it's not just a transition from call to success. That's what God is telling us. Life with God, Nate, isn't filled with calls and then victories. It's a call, and then it's a struggle. A big struggle just to hold on sometimes when promises don't come, and we run into big battles, and people fall off to the side. We try to edit out so many of the difficult parts so we can talk about God's victories. But, Nate, the Bible isn't so much about God's victories from what I can tell. Most of it's not about victory at all. It's about struggle, and it's the people who believe in God the most—who have the most faith—who have to go through these struggles. Not because God loves to see us hurt or squirming or in pain; it's because that's what life involves and God lets us experience life, all while telling us that, at the end, he wins over darkness.

"That's it," Joseph continues. "It's not us who wins, it's God who wins and we have to struggle along and trust that he's actually going to win. That's faith. That's the faith of Abraham. It's not the faith that brings us fame and money and one lovely thing after another; it's the faith that means holding onto God no matter what because this whole thing—this whole game we're in—is bigger and longer and deeper than we can possibly realize, and we're playing a part that means everything to us and yet there's so much more than us. The point is in the middle of the stories, Nate. Not the beginning or the end. That's what I missed; that's what I skipped over; that's what no one ever told me and what I had to learn on my own. Either that or I'd die because I couldn't live without Maggie any other way. I had to see there was something bigger—something that explained what Maggie went through, what I went through with her—but that told me all we went through wasn't meaningless. Wasn't the end. I saw it as the end. And it wasn't the end. The end was the beginning; the end is the beginning, and that's what you have to see too. That's what your congregation needs to hear, so they can start real discipleship while living in the middle of it all and so develop real faith." Joseph stops and takes a drink of water, holding the glass on his lips for a long moment after his sip. "Sorry. I got going and now I'm out of breath."

"That's okay. 'Once a pastor,' right?"

"Once a pastor," Joseph laughs. "Hard to break the old habits."

"Especially since those habits are what got us into the business in the first place," Nate replies.

"Probably so. But I think I said all I have to say in too short a burst. Did you understand any of that? Are you hearing what I'm getting at?"

"I think I am, Joe. And it makes sense. I wasn't looking at Scripture right. Old habit."

"It's part of the training, Nate. Part of the training I had and you had. We're supposed to tell people all the right things, how big God is, how great, how sovereign. But life isn't like that and so we try to squeeze life into our little theology of who we think God should be because that's who we think we need God to be. Only that's not who God says he is, and he tells us all through Scripture what to expect. But we don't want that, so we ignore those middle parts. We think we need someone who is above it all—putting everything in an order so we just follow the rails and go into our success."

"Like Autopia."

"What's that?"

"Disney ride. Drive little cars around the track. You have a steering wheel and a brake pedal and an accelerator. But you are on a track that keeps the car along the right path. You can bump against the rail, but not enough to really go anywhere else. It's very safe and orderly. Everyone goes on the same path. Everyone sees the same thing."

"Sure, sure, that's what we want from God. A Disney God. Easily described and packaged and marketed to everyone. But God isn't a Disney character. And the Christian life isn't a ride at Disneyland. It's messy. There are long stretches without even a single song. And it involves hurt, and battles, and suffering, and waiting so much longer than we think we should, and losing what we thought we absolutely needed. And that's just when we're really doing Christianity right. That's life. God doesn't save us from all of that, and he doesn't always cause that. I don't think—I can't think—that God made breast cancer and thought one day that he would take Maggie away from me just so I could be a better Christian. What I think is that there is breast cancer, Maggie died, and God still expected me to have faith, because Maggie's death isn't the end. It's not the end of me, and it's not the end of her. It's something along the way. And God is bigger than it and calls me to be bigger than it. Not so I can forget it or dismiss that pain, but so I can somehow teach others, and learn to really see what God is about in this world."

"Which is? How do you describe what God is about, Joe?"

"God is about relationship. He wants the whole world to be in relationship with him. He wants each of us to be in a real relationship with him throughout eternity. And that's a process. We all participate in ways: outreach, evangelism, service, reaching out. But if we're not getting ourselves and others into a real relationship with God, it's all a waste. And a relationship is hard work. It's a long, arduous, sometimes heartbreaking process, especially for those of us who just have to trust that the end is *his* end. It's a love affair with all the ups and downs and development."

"The end is his end," Nate responds. "I like that."

"Abraham's end was a beginning—the beginning of the Jewish people and the beginning of a journey. His struggles, his fight, were only a part of something so much bigger. This man of faith was called and then he had to fight, and wait, and wait so much longer. Then he had to struggle some more, fight some more, and even then he didn't see it all."

"I want you to tell me about Abraham, Joe. I feel like hearing the story again myself, maybe again for the first time. Maybe that's just what I need. Just to listen for a while. But I'm feeling like I need a night of rest first."

Over the next two days Joseph and Nate talk about Abraham and other things, then Nate drives back down the mountain, not entirely sure he's found any answers. But at least he knows how to better start looking.

"Maybe instead of asking 'Why do bad things happen to good people?' we should ask, 'What do good people do when bad things happen?'"

6

when bad times hit good people

"Sorry I'm late," Lisa says as she walks between the bookshelves to the table where Nate and Karl are sitting, each with a half-empty coffee in front of them.

"No problem," Nate replies. "Have a seat. How's the teaching business?"

"Feels like hard work and way too often totally meaningless," Lisa replies. "I guess I'm just feeling like it's a constant battle. We're fighting against so many other things in the students' lives that are sucking them away from their potential. Making them anonymous, like Melissa would say."

"They're lucky to have you, Lisa," Karl says. "Let me buy you something to drink."

"A nonfat chai would be absolutely divine. Thanks, Karl." Lisa settles into the chair.

Karl gets up and goes to the counter in the other part of the bookstore.

"I was on my way out the door, had everything put away, and one of my students walked in the door and said, 'Miss

McKee, I need to talk.' I was so surprised I couldn't tell him no. I got a little mad in second period because he was acting up a bit and hadn't done his homework. He wanted to apologize. So we talked about what had happened, and got to talking more about some steps he can take—we can take—to help him do better. His parents don't speak any English at all and he's been having real troubles with his essay assignments in general. I think there's a lot more going on, too, but he doesn't say much. He's really a good kid, and a good student if he can focus and just get his work done. I think he's really gifted, but is hitting this crossroads where he will either become a great student or a thug. Lots of influences tugging at him and I honestly don't know which way he'll go. So I feel I should do what little I can. Sorry, that was probably more than you wanted to know."

"The Spirit has you doing this key work at a key point in these kids' lives," Nate says. "It's beautiful."

"It doesn't feel very beautiful sometimes," Lisa replies. She sighs heavily, leans back in her chair, closes her eyes for a long moment, opens them. "How is Melissa doing?"

"Doing better. Debbie has been spending a lot of time over there and they seem to have become real close. I get the sense they are helping each other work things out."

"Don't need Pastor Nate at all," Lisa laughs. "Nice. I'm going by the hospital this weekend when I get a spare hour or two. How was your time up in the mountains? Did you have a mountaintop experience? I wouldn't mind one of those."

"Karl and I were just talking about that. I can't figure out if I did or didn't, you know?"

"What did you talk about?"

"Joe is this great guy. Older man, long-time pastor. His wife died a while back and that pushed him into this faith crisis. He left everything and moved to the mountains. Started reading the Bible again, this time without having to prepare a sermon or counsel anyone, or without needing to have any specific reason. Just read the Bible. We talked about that."

"About what he found?"

"Here you go," Karl says. He hands Lisa the tall, steaming cup and sits down, turning the chair as he does to give his long legs more room to stretch out. Karl Klaussen is in his late twenties, an on-and-off again college student, and a little more consistent guitar player now in his fourth band in seven years. His guitar-playing skill guaranteed he would have a musical role during gatherings, which led him into being the worship leader at the Upper Room, if such a role was actually defined. It's something he enjoys more than the concerts, truth be told.

"Thanks, Karl. This is a lifesaver," Lisa says after taking a sip.

"Joe talked about what he found," Nate continues, "but more specifically we talked about Abraham. How God worked in his life and the path he had for him."

"For four days? That's what you talked about?"

"That's what I said!" Karl exclaims.

"Basically. I mean we talked about other things too. And I took part in a gathering he has every week with some others in the area."

"What kind of gathering?" Karl asks.

"Well, apparently, about two years after he moved up there he realized he kept running into people who were fed up with a lot of church stuff, but really were seeking God. They felt alone and lost. Joe and these people started having a weekly conversation at Village Coffee, where they could sit as long as they wanted, getting refills of what really is some of the best freshly roasted coffee I've tasted. The owners, Mike and Jean Sherry—I met them when we stopped by—would occasionally join in. So would other people. Soon they were taking up half the tables or more. Joe doesn't call it a church or anything special, but it sounds a lot like what we're doing with the Upper Room. They've been meeting for about fifteen years or so."

"Fifteen years?" Lisa asks. "I thought we were doing something new!"

"Ha!" Nate laughs. "New to us, I guess. I made the same point. Joe laughed and said, 'What? You think you're the first one the Spirit has ever worked in? God works, Nate, in a lot of places, even if he doesn't always get newspaper and magazine advertisements about the work.' I laughed."

"So what did you learn?" Lisa asks. "Any decisions? Any new insights?"

"A lot," Nate replies, "but nothing settled. It's all still rattling around in my head. And that's kind of what I'm wanting to talk more about—with everyone."

"So you're staying?" Karl asks.

"Honestly, I don't know," Nate replies. "I don't know where I'm landing with that yet. I decided not to decide, and instead wait for something more clear. I thought I knew. But I keep going back and forth. A buddy from San Diego called me yesterday, out of the blue. Hadn't talked to him for years. He and his wife have started a small church plant. Same kind of thing we're doing here. They're having a lot of real great response and he wanted to know if I would come down and join in. We used to be real close, and we did a lot of work—church work—together back in the day. Sounds like just the sign I was looking for. Looking for before I went up to Big Bear. Now? I don't know. And if I don't know, I don't want to decide. I want to wrestle with this—with what I learned from Joe, with what is going on in our community. I'm tired of the same old discussions and same old answers. I want to go deeper."

"Like you want to figure out how you're feeling," Lisa says.

"I suspect I'm not the only one. So, I want to see what this means for me. For us."

"There is something," Karl says. "I've felt it, too, but I haven't had any idea how to express what it is. So what are you thinking, Nate?"

"I've been reading through the first books of the Bible again and I think there's a lot to chew on."

"Where do we begin?" Lisa asks.

"God got Israel to Egypt," Nate replies. "But then he left. Went silent. God went silent. It's weird. But it's what he did."

"Makes me think about Jesus in the garden," Karl says.

"How so?" Lisa asks.

"There he is, praying, sweating blood he's so stressed, crying out to the Father. But where's the Father?"

"He knew the Father was there," Lisa says.

"I think the Israelites did too," Nate replies. "They just didn't know why he wasn't responding. They knew to cry out to him. They remembered him. They kept crying out. Even if God was silent they kept crying out."

"Why was God silent?" Karl asks. "Was it something they did?"

"That's the question," Nate says. "We can't just say that if bad things are happening it's because of sin. Sometimes we can. Sometimes that's exactly it. But so much of the church has tried to follow the simple logic: 'If you do bad things, bad things happen'; 'Do good things and good things happen.' But this isn't necessarily the case. That's why I'm so intrigued with Exodus. I mean look how it opens. Everything is going great."

> ▶ These are the names of the sons of Israel who went to Egypt with Jacob, each with his family: Reuben, Simeon, Levi and Judah; Issachar, Zebulun and Benjamin; Dan and Naphtali; Gad and Asher. The descendants of Jacob numbered seventy in all; Joseph was already in Egypt.
>
> Now Joseph and all his brothers and all that generation died, but the Israelites were fruitful and multiplied greatly and became exceedingly numerous, so that the land was filled with them.
> (Exodus 1:1-7)   Ω

"What were they doing wrong?" Nate asks.

"Nothing," Lisa answers. "Joseph was faithful to God and his family was saved because of how God had worked in his life."

"His earlier, prophetic dreams came true," Karl adds. "Though with a bit of struggle there in the middle. But God worked. And everything was blessed."

"Exactly," Nate laughs. "We can't poke holes in this. There's nothing in this passage to say that they're doing anything wrong, or that anything evil is happening. It's saying that the family of Israel is right with God. But then it shifts. In a weird direction. We know the story so well we don't realize how really strange it is."

> ▶ Then a new king, who did not know about Joseph, came to power in Egypt. "Look," he said to his people, "the Israelites have become much too numerous for us. Come, we must deal shrewdly with them or they will become even more numerous and, if war breaks out,

> will join our enemies, fight against us and
> leave the country."
> (Exodus 1:8-10)

Ω

"Why is it strange?" Lisa asks.

"Because of what we expect next. The Israelites have been walking right. God has been working. We see something like this and then we expect a quick miracle, like all the Israelites get swords and fight off their Egyptian oppressors. Or that Pharaoh dies and a new one comes into power, this one who remembers Joseph. Or maybe, '…and from among the people rose up an Israelite leader who overcame the slavery and brought peace to all of Egypt.'"

"Well, there was Moses," Lisa says.

"But that's not what comes next," Nate replies. "That's what I'm getting at. We skip the middle. The hard parts. The parts that talk about struggle. We don't want to dwell on those parts. We want the victory. The success."

"Isn't that faith?" Karl asks. "We hold onto the hope?"

"Not really," Lisa answers. "I think I'm getting what you're saying, Nate. If we skip to the end too quickly we lose how really serious the struggle is. And then we forget there is a struggle, which keeps us from seeing a relationship between the story and our lives. Because I don't know the end. In *Technicolor Dreamcoat*, Joseph is in prison but they don't sit with that for long. Instead, they show a little of his woe, and then he's surrounded by people saying it's all going to be alright. They've read the end, I think the narrator sings. Only that's not the case with me. I don't have a narrator following me around."

"That's the struggle I'm feeling too," Nate says. "I really don't know what direction to take next. I'm feeling a lot of frustration but what does that mean?"

"We want to blame something," Lisa says. "Blame ourselves. Or come up with a reason—something that could have been changed or could help us next time."

"But like with Melissa," Karl adds, "what could have been changed? Those kinds of things can happen almost anywhere, and it's almost like plain bad luck."

"Wrong place, wrong time," Lisa adds.

"And the only way to prevent bad things from happening is to hide," Karl says. "Let fear win. Give up and hide, or give in, totally ruined, and think that those bad circumstances are truth."

"That's what is so powerful about this early part of Exodus for me," Nate says. "Unlike the prophets, who give the reasons and give warnings, all we see here is unprovoked anger. There's no cause. Israel was blessed. Egypt was blessed. Everyone was blessed with God's work."

"Which turns everything around," Lisa says.

"What do you mean?" Karl asks.

"Like Nate said, the prophets are talking about curses—what happens when people do something wrong. Only that's not it here. And that seems to be the point. The oppression came, not because they were cursed or doing something wrong. Seems like Egypt's response came from jealousy. And fear. Because God's promise was being worked out."

"It was because they were within God's path of promise," Nate continues, "and Egypt responded by taking control."

> ▶ So they put slave masters over them to oppress them with forced labor, and they built Pithom and Rameses as store cities for Pharaoh. But the more they were oppressed, the more they multiplied and spread; so the Egyptians came to dread the Israelites and worked them ruthlessly. They made their lives bitter with hard labor in brick and mortar and with all

> kinds of work in the fields; in all their hard labor the Egyptians used them ruthlessly.
> (Exodus 1:11-14)
>
> Ω

"The Egyptian king didn't remember Joseph, so he didn't know what God had done in helping Egypt in time of famine," Nate continued. "And he inflicted evil, undeserved evil, on the people. He noticed their blessings, noticed their qualities, and it made him furious."

"But God still was working," Lisa says. "That's what gets me about this verse. The Egyptians tried to throw everything at the Israelites. They 'made their lives bitter with hard labor.' Life was hard. But it didn't change the fact that God was still working."

"Like Joseph did in prison," Karl says. "He was a blessing to others in the jail even as everything must have felt like a curse to him. God was working, but it sure didn't seem like it."

"But God was working even more," Lisa says, "when it seemed Joseph was going through the worst. I mean, that really sounds strange, but I can't help thinking that the isolation and the frustration put Joseph in the position to help when the time was ripe."

"I think this is where real faith comes in," Nate says. "Faith didn't change anything, I mean we could even say things got worse and worse. But faith transformed the situation. The oppression wasn't better, but it wasn't meaningless either. The faith gave meaning. A lot of faith isn't about what happens in the future. It's about how we see what is happening to us in the present."

"But isn't that just putting a good spin on things?" Lisa asks. "Optimism. What if we don't have any optimism left? What if we just feel the ruthlessness of it all so heavily we feel we can't go on?"

"God was working through them," Nate says. "They were still blessed, even though the very blessing was the source of their pain. They grew in numbers, even still. The persecution wasn't enough to offset God's plans, even though I know those people felt so abandoned and so crushed, wondering where God was in their pain."

"Reminds me of the early church," Karl adds. "Acts is full of these stories. Stephen is martyred. The church grows. James is beheaded. The church grows. Saul goes on a rampage, and the church is scattered. Then it grows in all sorts of places, and Saul becomes Paul, the greatest missionary."

"'The blood of martyrs is the seed of the church,'" Nate says.

"'Blessed are the poor in Spirit,'" Lisa says. "I have seen that as being a consolation. The poor and depressed and whoever else don't have anything to show for their labor and suffering, so they feel like they have their rewards in heaven. But what you're saying explains it better to me. These people God has chosen are the people who are being particularly oppressed. What if we had forgotten the story of Joseph too? And came to Exodus without knowing anything of the promise to Abraham? All we would see is a bunch of low-class people having a lot of children. But we know the end of the story, so we can't see the Israelites as the people at the absolute bottom of society."

"God may be working the most among those who are most persecuted," Karl says. "They're the least and the lowest in their own cultures, but they might be very important for what God is doing in this world."

"Maybe," Nate says.

"Maybe." Karl pauses for a moment. "Maybe instead of asking 'Why do bad things happen to good people?' we should ask, 'What do good people do when bad things happen?'"

"I think you are exactly right," Lisa says. "We can't explain God or life or what happens to people. All we can do is explain what we're going to do about it—how we respond and how we choose to act."

"How we choose to act when we are attacked," Karl adds. "And even then, this is really hard for me. I mean, I get it, but it takes so much more from me than I think I have. When we respond right, we still can't expect everything to turn out right."

"Like with Joseph," Lisa says. "He served God and things got worse."

"Which is crazy," Nate says. "But that's what Scripture says. In Exodus the people are blessed by having more children. Only, the oppression doesn't just get irritating and then ease up. It gets worse. Even what they have—the increase in their families which is the one thing they can point to as being a sign of God's favor—is attacked. That's taken away from them."

> ▶ The king of Egypt said to the Hebrew midwives, whose names were Shiphrah and Puah, "When you help the Hebrew women in childbirth and observe them on the delivery stool, if it is a boy, kill him; but if it is a girl, let her live." The midwives, however, feared God and did not do what the king of Egypt had told them to do; they let the boys live. Then the king of Egypt summoned the midwives and asked them, "Why have you done this? Why have you let the boys live?"
>
> The midwives answered Pharaoh, "Hebrew women are not like Egyptian women; they are vigorous and give birth before the midwives arrive."
>
> So God was kind to the midwives and the people increased and became even more numerous. And because the midwives feared God, he gave them families of their own.

> Then Pharaoh gave this order to all his people: "Every boy that is born you must throw into the Nile, but let every girl live."
> (Exodus 1:15-22)

Ω

"The one thing, the one thing the people could point to," Nate continues. "What may have been the one joy in their lives—having children—is taken away from them. We focus on the miracles that come later. We focus on the victories and the triumphs. But pause here and everything is dark. Boy children are being drowned in the Nile! Where is God as these babies are slaughtered?"

"That's a hard question," Lisa answers. "He's with them. Because we know they didn't die out but were saved."

"We know that," Nate replies. "But think of how it feels in the moment. Here—here in Exodus—God is telling the story that defeat and attacks aren't the whole story. They are included within the story."

"I remember being out of work for a year," Karl says, "a few years after high school. Almost on the street many times. No one would interview me. No one would call me back. Each time I submitted an application it went with hope and prayer. And then the silence slowly beat me down. I did have music. But when the guitar strings broke, I couldn't justify going out to buy more. I had to pawn my guitar. I was really depressed. God stopped me, and I couldn't do anything to move forward. Nothing worked. Then it seemed what I did have was taken away. I couldn't distract myself from the frustration.

"What words would have been comforting to you?" Nate asks.

"Honestly, nothing," Karl replies. "Answers. That was the only real comfort."

"But you kept trying," Lisa says.

"Yeah, I did keep doing what I could. My thought was that even if I was cursed or whatever, I wasn't going to give an excuse. Honestly, I was challenging God. I was saying he wasn't going to provoke me to becoming my own problem."

"Which is what the midwives did," Nate says. "They didn't follow the orders. They lied to Pharaoh. And this lying wasn't to protect themselves. It was, I think, an assertion of the promise. They were holding God to his promise. They weren't going to let the promise go, even as everything was being taken away."

"And they were blessed because of it," Lisa says. "Because even when everything was wrong, they didn't just lie down and let the babies die. They fought. They held on. God blessed them for it."

"Then Pharaoh stepped up again," Nate says. "He told all his people that they had to throw the baby boys into the river. He wouldn't take any excuse. He was ruthless. Insulting. Absolutely crushing. Where was God?"

"I don't know," Karl answers. "It doesn't make sense to me. Seems like infanticide is enough reason for God to step in. But he doesn't."

"Not right away," Lisa says.

Both Moses and his mother faced unendurable circumstances. She voluntarily let go—put her son into God's hands. She had no power and hardly any resources, while Moses had everything. And then he tried to fix a problem by using force. He tried to fix it himself.

7

when it's time to let go

"Why would there be traffic now?" Luke asks. "It's eleven in the morning. Where are these people going?" The white Toyota truck on their right starts to merge into their lane, without really waiting for space to do so. Luke doesn't try to prove anything, coming to a stop on the 101 as traffic inches farther forward ahead of him and the white Toyota moves over. "Why aren't they at work?" he asks with mock seriousness, trying to find a sense of humor. He skipped breakfast this morning and is starting to get a little hungry, not the best situation while in stop-and-go traffic, still an hour from their destination.

After a month of very long work hours for both of them, Luke and Heather Jouvenet decided they needed a long weekend away, and Santa Barbara was both close and far enough for such an escape. A lot was going on and they hardly had any time just as a couple. One thing they learned over the years—made clear when their marriage was on the brink of failure—was that they couldn't write off spending time together. They had to make time for each other a priority, otherwise cracks formed in their relationship.

They also had decisions to make, and the scattered conversations in the comings and goings of their lives provided no answers. They had been trying to have a baby for almost a year-and-a-half. In their mid-thirties they felt everything in life was primed for an expanding household. They both very much wanted children. This was the time, they thought. Only no baby came. Recent visits with a fertility doctor revealed what could be known and what remained mystery. The known parts had variably successful medical responses. The mysterious parts still had prayer. They decided they needed focused time to figure it out.

"Maybe instead of seeing this traffic as a delay, we should make good use of our time," Heather suggests.

"I could dictate an article about the need for highway expansion," Luke replies.

"So sarcastic," Heather says. "No, something actually helpful. I'm thinking about what we talked about at the gathering this last Sunday."

"About what?"

"Like what did Moses' mom think?" Heather asks. "I can't imagine what she felt like, what any of the mothers felt like. Knowing at any moment their sons would be snatched from their arms. Moses' mother devised a plan. But she still had to let go." Heather opens the bag at her feet and pulls out her Bible, turning the pages to the beginning of Exodus. "I'll read. We'll talk. Make this a fruitful drive. A good lesson for you."

"Likely so," Luke laughs. "Likely so. Especially if this truck in front keeps increasing his following distance." He feels the frustration build. "If you're going to get in my lane, go with the flow," he complains out loud.

"Shhh. I'm going to read now," Heather says. "You listen."

> ▶ Now a man of the house of Levi married a Levite woman, and she became pregnant and gave birth to a son. When she saw that he was a fine child, she hid him for three months. But when she could hide him no longer, she got a

> papyrus basket for him and coated it with tar and pitch. Then she placed the child in it and put it among the reeds along the bank of the Nile. His sister stood at a distance to see what would happen to him.
> (Exodus 2:1-4)
>
> Ω

"Pushed to the absolute edge," Heather continues. "The moment of joy—It's a boy!—followed almost immediately by the need to figure out some way to save his life."

"The Egyptians would come to kill him," Luke says, falling into the quick change of conversation. Over the last year, they had made a point of regular devotions together and more purposeful, deeper conversations. They realized that early in their marriage they assumed a level of depth that was never really there. At first their attempts to establish a more intimate relationship felt weird and uncomfortable—they had gotten out of the habit of these kinds of deeper conversations. But they stuck with the discipline, and found parts of their hearts opening up like never before. Now, they fell into these kinds of conversations easily.

"No doubt the pharaoh made sure people followed his rules," Heather says. "Last Saturday, while you were at work, I watched a History Channel show about the Nazis in Poland. If someone was found hiding Jewish men or women, they were killed. Not only them, but often their whole family and sometimes the whole village. I wouldn't doubt that same kind of brutality was here too. I mean, it's crazy, isn't it? They were attacked because they were numerous and successful. Just like in Germany four thousand years later. And like Jesus too. With Herod. Herod killed all the babies in Bethlehem, looking for Jesus, because he was supposed to be the next king. All those babies died because of that fear. I wonder if any mothers were able to hide their children from the Romans like Moses' mom hid him."

"They all hid Moses. It wasn't just her. They all stood together. No one said anything."

"I wonder what happened?" Heather asks.

"What happened with what?" Luke replies.

"What made it too difficult to keep hiding him. Three months. And then that was it. Something happened. They couldn't keep hiding him."

"Their whole lives were thrown into chaos. Young married couples. What would they think? How many wouldn't take the risk of becoming pregnant? What would we think? Every little bit of joy and privacy was taken away because of this. They couldn't get away from it. And you're right. Something must have happened, made their situation untenable."

"What?"

"They couldn't keep hiding him, like you said. There was a breaking point. A mom, a family, risked their lives for three months because of the threat to their child. But then they had to do something."

"It got worse than we know. Something happened."

"This Jewish mother did something that must have absolutely broken her heart. She couldn't do anything more. So she let go. And that's it, isn't it? She had to just let go. They had forced the situation this far, and now it was too much. They couldn't force anything else. She had to let Moses go. And she did it. She couldn't keep hold of him, and so she had to just let it all go."

"Put it in God's hands," Heather says.

"Yeah," Luke replies. "Though I wonder how she thought of that." The traffic comes to a complete stop. Even the carpool lane is no longer moving. Luke tries to look around the Ford F-150 in front of him, but can't see past it. Most of the people in the other cars are talking on cell phones, probably to explain why they are late to whomever is waiting at their destination. Except for the guy behind them. At first, Luke thinks he is angry at something. Then he realizes the guy is singing along to the radio. Complete with hand gestures. "Look behind us."

"What?"

"Just glance."

Heather looks, and then quickly turns back when the guy catches her eye. She tries to stifle her laugh, but doesn't entirely succeed.

"*That's* a good use of time," Luke laughs. "So, anyway....I totally forgot what I was saying."

"Moses being let go," Heather reminds him.

"Right!" Luke says. "There must have been a sliver of faith left…in someone or something. But where had God been up to now, right? Moses' mom had to trust, she had to let go, knowing that everything had gotten worse up to that point. What could she expect would happen next?"

"She had no other choice."

"That's it, isn't it? She had no choice. It wasn't a choice really. She had to let go of the whole situation. She—all of them—did what they could do and they came to some kind of wall, where they couldn't do anything more. Imagine being in that situation."

"I can't. I can't imagine what that would have felt like. What it would have felt like to make the basket. Then put Moses into it. 'Shhhhhh, Moses….Shhhhh…don't cry.' Then she hands the basket to her daughter. 'Put this in the river.' Why didn't she go herself?"

"Maybe she was being watched," Luke says. "There were suspicions. If Moses was found he would have been killed, and the sister would have been killed, most likely."

"If she had held onto Moses more tightly, I wonder what would have happened?"

"If she hadn't put him in the river? They would have been caught at some point. Everything would have been lost. Their hope, their only hope, was that she didn't hold too tight. That's crazy. I mean, I hold too tight on a news story. Too tight on whether my coffee is made right in the morning. She had to let go of her own baby boy and trust that it was going to be okay. She couldn't force this situation. Nothing was getting better. So she had to let him go."

"God told her to let her baby go."

"Where was God?" Luke asks. "Where did they see God? Boys were being slaughtered. Cast adrift as the last bit of hope. The Hebrews were slaves, beaten and crushed. Everything was going wrong. So where was God?"

"On the bank of the river," Heather answers. "Right?"

"What do you mean?"

"The sister saw where God was. On the bank of the river."

> ▶ Then Pharaoh's daughter went down to the Nile to bathe, and her attendants were walking along the river bank. She saw the basket among the reeds and sent her slave girl to get it. She opened it and saw the baby. He was crying, and she felt sorry for him. "This is one of the Hebrew babies," she said.
>
> Then his sister asked Pharaoh's daughter, "Shall I go and get one of the Hebrew women to nurse the baby for you?"
>
> "Yes, go," she answered. And the girl went and got the baby's mother. Pharaoh's daughter said to her, "Take this baby and nurse him for me, and I will pay you." So the woman took the baby and nursed him. When the child grew

> older, she took him to Pharaoh's daughter and he became her son. She named him Moses, saying, "I drew him out of the water."
> (Exodus 2:5-10)
>
> Ω

"Moses' sister watched him go," Heather says. "Let him go, like you said. And he floated all the way down to Pharaoh's daughter."

"The daughter of the man who ordered all the boy babies killed."

"Yeah. I mean, who knows what his daughter was going to do? Imagine the sister watching all of that. Everything was hanging in that balance. She says a little prayer. A last little prayer. She stays to watch, can't look away. She can't see God anywhere. But there he is, in front of her. The daughter doesn't care about daddy's orders. 'This is one of the Hebrew babies,' she says. I wonder what her story was? She had such compassion. We're not told anything more about her, though."

"God *was* there," Luke says. "He had worked in this daughter, in Pharaoh's daughter. Everything came together at this moment. Whatever issues the daughter had with her father played into it. She felt sorrow, not anger. How many Egyptians had the same response to Pharaoh's orders? Evil had taken control but that doesn't mean evil was everywhere. God had been working. And we see this quiet, gentle, unmiraculous moment. I mean, it's no big deal. It's this beautiful little scene. Something like, 'Amidst the gently swaying reeds of the languid Nile River, a baby floated. In between life and death.' I might even think there's a story in this somewhere." He laughs. "Though who would have noticed? Just a little baby. Where was God? Where was the miracle of salvation for the whole Jewish people? It's all there. The whole of Genesis narrows us into this little basket floating lazily down a river until it bumps up against an Egyptian princess."

The traffic starts to move along more quickly, and Luke and Heather get up to about thirty miles an hour. Luke smiles a bit, wishing the Toyota just in front of him would not take quite as much time to build speed.

"It's perfect," Heather says. "Who else would have defied the king?"

"Who else? That's right. It is so subtle. Elegant. What if the current was going a little too fast? Or she had gotten distracted? Crazy to think about how much went into this seemingly innocuous little story. God is all through it, isn't he? Where is God? You hit it, Heather, he was on the bank of the Nile, waiting and working. Just enough. Just enough for this moment—the moment that would lead to so many more moments. All the moments of the rest of the Bible."

"We want the obvious, big miracle," Heather says. "The instant salvation. Something like, 'And Pharaoh declared he was wrong and all the babies were to live! And so Moses grew up and became a healthy male working in the brick factory. That would have been a great story. Only we wouldn't have heard of it. Not at all. All the pressure, everything that happened, wasn't by accident. It was leading somewhere. To a different outcome than they expected."

"A different outcome?" Luke asks.

"I mean, Moses' mom just wanted Moses to live. That's what she prayed for. How it worked out, with all the tragedy, meant there was a bigger, much bigger, story going on. It was like the evil was turned into this huge, great thing. 'And we know that in all things God works for the good of those who love him, who have been called according to his purpose.'"

"Romans 8:28," Luke says. "Yeah. Worked for good."

"See, I know a Bible verse!" Heather laughs.

"There is hope for this world, yet," Luke replies, also with a laugh.

"But doesn't that sound trite? The verse, I mean."

"What do you mean?"

"I guess I'm terrible for saying this," Heather answers. "But that verse just seems so trite. Good for Moses, sure. But what about all the other mothers? What about all the other baby boys that didn't float down the river and find a princess. What about those who ended up at the bottom of the river? What about their good?"

"I've never thought about the rest."

Traffic slows. No seeming reason, not even a curve in the freeway. Just slows to about fifteen miles an hour.

"And yet they're all in this story too," Heather continues, much less irritated than Luke by every random speed shift. "This isn't just about Moses. It's about all the Hebrews. All of them. So where are they left?"

"But I don't see how this changes anything," Luke says.

"I mean, Moses wasn't just saved for himself and for his mother. *Everyone* was waiting for God's salvation. Not only for themselves. For their whole families, for their future. And God was working. Only it wasn't the immediate work they wanted. I guess that's where I run into a wall."

"I guess," Luke says, "even what they saw as their end wasn't the end. God was doing something bigger, something for all the generations. If they could hold onto that, I suppose, it made more sense. They were part of something; their lives weren't isolated.

"But where does that leave us?" Heather asks. "I guess that's what I'm asking myself. What if *we're* not the people who find a princess but the ones who only find the loss?"

"I don't know," Luke says. He doesn't say anything else for a few moments. The singing guy behind him has changed lanes and is now passing them on their right, no longer singing. "I guess we see God is working through all sorts of stories. It was the Spirit, right, who was working in the princess? That tied everything together in this elegant way. The Spirit was working, even in the midst of tragedy."

"So, it's like, what do *we* know?"

"Yeah, just like that. What do we know about the big picture? That leaves me with a couple of thoughts, I suppose. One is that we just have to trust that what we see isn't everything. God is working toward his own end. We're part of something bigger and more thorough."

"What's the second thought?"

They come to a complete stop. Farther ahead there's only the slightest movement. This is going to be a long drive. They haven't even got out of L.A. County yet. Luke's mind wanders before he catches himself and thinks about her question.

"Ha!" Luke laughs, "I forgot."

"Well, I better keep reading," Heather says and laughs with him. "Maybe it'll pop back in. So, Moses is raised by his own mother. Everything worked out because she totally let go. She let go and had her son. And he had more privilege than any other Hebrew."

"Best of both worlds."

"But not really, right? I mean look what comes next."

> ▶ One day, after Moses had grown up, he went out to where his own people were and watched them at their hard labor. He saw an Egyptian beating a Hebrew, one of his own people. Glancing this way and that and seeing no one, he killed the Egyptian and hid him in the sand. The next day he went out and saw

> two Hebrews fighting. He asked the one in the wrong, "Why are you hitting your fellow Hebrew?"
>
> The man said, "Who made you ruler and judge over us? Are you thinking of killing me as you killed the Egyptian?" Then Moses was afraid and thought, "What I did must have become known."
>
> When Pharaoh heard of this, he tried to kill Moses, but Moses fled from Pharaoh and went to live in Midian, where he sat down by a well.
> *(Exodus 2:11-15)* Ω

"Everything," Heather continues, "had been totally out of their control. Moses' mother got to the very end of things and even then had to let go. Totally powerless. Had to trust the currents and the water... and the Egyptian princess."

"So Moses grows up. He's given everything, I mean everything. He had his real mother and all the benefits of the Hebrew world, and then he had all the success, training, education of being raised in the Egyptian royal household. Moses had probably the best childhood of any Hebrew around. Everything was given to him. It was all turning out great. But there was still a major problem."

"The hard labor?" Heather asks.

"Yes. Moses being saved wasn't the answer. Not for the real problem. It was nice and all, but nothing had changed. Moses had everything going for him. This Hebrew was a victorious, free Hebrew. But he was still enslaved. Because his people were still being brutally treated. He was left with feeling the joy of his own freedom while being enslaved by others' lack of freedom."

"It made him an angry man."

"That's it," Luke replies. "Totally. Instead of rejoicing he became angry, violent even. His own salvation meant nothing. So he had to act. Had to do something. He was saved, right, so had to go out and make a difference. Only it wasn't God's work. It wasn't God's plan. Moses got it all wrong. But he was active. And so it must have felt so righteous to respond, to throw a blow for God's kingdom, right?"

"I bet he felt so satisfied afterward, like he made this major stance."

"A stance for himself though, right? Not for God. To cure his own guilt of being saved while others weren't. But it wasn't about God. And that seems to be so much of what these stories are about. It's always about God. Always. Time. Space. Victory. Hope. It all is about God. But we get caught up in our own stories and forget that. And then we're not as effective. We feel what we feel and respond to the problem, doing what we want to do—what feels good in the moment. It distracts us from the bigger picture."

Traffic again starts picking up. Space opens up in the far left lane and Luke moves into it, accelerating past the Toyota that seems to think fifty-five is still the speed limit. He looks over as he drives past and sees a younger man using one hand to hold his cell phone to his ear.

"So what does all this say to us?" Heather asks.

"I'm thinking it's about letting go. Both Moses and his mother faced unendurable circumstances. She voluntarily let go—put her son into God's hands."

Heather sees what's next and jumps in. "She had no power and hardly any resources, while Moses had everything."

"Exactly," Luke says, "and he tried to take more, take it by force, make what was afflicting him go away because he couldn't stand it. He tried to fix it himself. Force the situation."

"We do try to force it," Heather says. "Tell God what to do and when to do it. Only we see *our* picture, not the *big* picture." She stops as they come to a complete stop again, and hears muttering from Luke. "Get behind me, Satan!" she yells.

"What?"

"From the Gospels. Jesus says he's going to be crucified. Peter tells Jesus not to talk like that."

"Talk like what?" Luke says, knowing what he muttered, and thinking he didn't say it that loudly.

"Not to discourage the big picture," Heather says.

"Right," Luke replies, getting back to the conversation. "Yeah. That's so interesting isn't it? Why he calls him 'Satan.' Peter is telling Jesus not to follow God, basically—to take matters into his own hands. The cross is so passive, right? Jesus is the victim, and Peter can't see Jesus as the victim. But it's the failure of the cross—what seems like a failure, I mean—that ends up meaning so much more."

"And Moses went from being this self-imposed hero to being a failure."

"Yeah," Luke replies. "His moment of seeming triumph. His strike against *The Man*, right? Not only is it bad for his relationship with the Egyptians, the Hebrews don't trust him. He is caught between and has to flee. He had everything, tried to force it all, and then lost it all. He had to leave everything he knew and run away."

"Funny to think that this is God's work. But it is, I suppose," Heather says.

"That's why it's so rare for people to carry on doing really good works. How many people have been like Mother Theresa? But really, how hard is it? Just let go of a lot and help people, right? Not hard at all. But hardly anyone really does that even though almost everyone celebrates it. Everyone has a wall. They hit it. It breaks them. They become just like everyone else. The crusade ends. They go back home without having conquered the castle."

"Yeah. Go back home a failure."

"Or like Moses," Luke says. "Driven from home. Somewhere I read, or maybe it was something Nate told me, about how so many attempts to do good come from really bad motives or really hollow souls. They see the *do-gooding* as a way to find themselves. It's not really giving. It's an attempt to find an identity. People who can't come to terms with themselves try to then fix other people. And it's what you said: Instead of helping they become a burden, a weight. Like Moses was, helping neither Egyptian nor Hebrew, becoming neither Egyptian nor Hebrew, right? People like that spread their own chaos, their own hollowness. It's all action. They don't know who to be."

"God wants us to act," Heather says, "but within him, for him, alongside him. Not out of our hollowness, but out of his fullness."

"What is his fullness for us?" Luke asks, turning and looking at Heather. She looks back at him, and he turns and looks back at the now nicely flowing freeway. "What do we do? If we act are we following God's will or trying to force our will?"

"That's what this weekend is about, I guess," she replies after a long moment. "We ask him and try to listen. That's all we can do, I suppose. All we can do right now."

They both look in different directions, enjoying finally getting out of the suburbs and into open spaces. They drive in a comfortable silence for a long while.

The Israelites groaned in their slavery and cried out, and their cry for help because of their slavery went up to God. God heard their groaning and he remembered his covenant with Abraham, with Isaac and with Jacob. So God looked on the Israelites and was concerned about them.

(Exodus 2:23-25)

8

when God hears the cries of his people

"What's funny to me, Nate," Ryan Gossett says, "is that you really were the first person I thought of. After all that happened. What you said then was what came to mind now. Even when I didn't understand it at the time. God has a sense of humor, I suppose."

"And his own way of doing things," Nate replies.

"That's for sure. That's for sure."

"So what's next?"

They sit outside in front of the Columba Pub and Restaurant, at one of the tables near the outer edge of the patio. Nate wears jeans probably six months past the time he should have thrown them out, and a T-shirt with Marc Chagall's "I and the Village" on the front. He last shaved about a week ago. Ryan is clean shaven, with short, conservatively cut, blondish hair, nicely pressed Dockers, and a short-sleeved, chartreuse button-down shirt. He sits up straight and looks uncomfortable, even though people often spend hours in the padded chairs. He hopes no one sees him at a pub like this.

As Ryan talks, he doesn't look at Nate. He focuses instead on a bird searching for crumbs, or the fluttering of the dark green awning above, especially when he says something more personal than he's used to revealing. And there has been a lot of that, especially after the first five minutes when Nate asked how Caroline was doing and what Ashley and Ethan were up to these days. When Nate last saw the kids they were both so young; Ethan had just been born. Now Ashley is eight and Ethan is five, both loving school. Learning that gave Nate a little shock, reminding him how much time has actually passed since his old life when he was connected with Ryan.

Nate used to work with Ryan, and before that they went to seminary together—were roommates in fact. Many hours—countless—they spent talking about ministry, theology, and all kinds of other church-related topics. Just never anything personal.

"I don't know what's next. You hiring?" Ryan asks.

"Ha! I'm not exactly sure I'm hired here myself," Nate replies. "And I'm definitely sure I don't have the power to hire anyone else. But I can't imagine you'd want to work here."

"No," Ryan admits in agreement. "I mean, I get what you're doing. Now, at least. But I don't know if I could do it—be so free and unprogrammed. I still like the programs. I guess that's really my problem. I like the events. I like the religion, Nate. I just don't really believe in God anymore. And now I'm stuck. It's not like I can get a job doing anything practical." He laughs but looks away without making eye contact with Nate.

"Is it burnout, you think? Or some kind of problem with God?"

"Is it me or my theology; is that what you're asking? I don't know. It's all tied together."

"Remember Chris Simpson?" Nate asks.

"Yeah! What happened to him?"

"Full scholarship to seminary. Everything paid. He gets through a year and a half, drops out halfway through the quarter. Fails all his classes. Scholarship is revoked. Last I heard he's working corporate sales at a computer company. Doing pretty well for himself, too, I heard."

"Doing pretty well for himself?" Ryan says, a bit wistfully. "Remember the conversations we had? Up to four in the morning talking Kant and Barth and so excited about ministry? What happened to us, Nate? Well, not you, you seemed to have somehow kept your feet. But I'm slipping here and I don't see bottom. I don't know what to say to anyone." He stops, lost in that thought, then continues, "I've got a mortgage now. A mortgage, can you believe it? I'm such a sellout. But it's the mortgage, not the ministry, that I care about." He stops, then asks, "How did you keep the faith?"

Nate doesn't respond right away, but instead takes a drink of water before answering. "For a time it felt like I did lose my faith in God. But I didn't really. I lost faith in the god I had, which wasn't really God. I didn't know why people didn't respond like they should, why they put all the pressure on me to do all the work. I wondered where God was. He wasn't there. Church work was just a whole lot of keeping people busy. Opiate of the masses And I was the dealer."

"Yeah," Ryan replies, now looking right at Nate. "That's it. That's it. Where is God? I've worked my butt off—pardon the language—and I feel more alone now than I ever did. I feel like I've run and run and fought and fought, and I'm left here, almost forty—almost forty can you believe it?—without anything in my soul, feeling like all I'm doing is putting my finger in a dam that's so cracked that it's going to collapse at any moment. The people don't want us, Nate. They say they do, and they show up, but they only want us to play our roles. Where's God in all of this?"

"This is going to sound so trite and religious, I know, but keep with me. You totally remind me of Moses."

"Moses?" Ryan laughs. "I'm not coming down from a mountain, Nate. I'm not leading anyone anywhere, and I'm certainly not chosen by God."

"Yeah, and that's what Moses thought too. We're going through Exodus now in our community. When was the last time you read Exodus?"

"Seminary, probably. Dr. Archer's class. Remember him? Barely could walk but when he talked about the law he was like a new man. Full of passion." Ryan pauses, wondering where that passion was for him. "It's been a while," he continues. "Not immediately relevant enough."

"Only it absolutely is," Nate replies.

"Absolutely is? How's that? How does Moses fit into this? With me?"

"Moses is a model for us. The whole story is. We've been told the story because we are supposed to learn from it, see it not only as a story but as a model, a true part of history that illustrates in a big way how God works."

"What does that mean?"

"Well," Nate says, as he leans over and pulls his Bible out of his backpack. "Maybe you've been fighting too long and you're not supposed to be fighting at all."

> ▶ One day, after Moses had grown up, he went out to where his own people were and watched them at their hard labor. He saw an Egyptian beating a Hebrew, one of his own people. Glancing this way and that and seeing

no one, he killed the Egyptian and hid him in the sand. The next day he went out and saw two Hebrews fighting. He asked the one in the wrong, "Why are you hitting your fellow Hebrew?" The man said, "Who made you ruler and judge over us? Are you thinking of killing me as you killed the Egyptian?" Then Moses was afraid and thought, "What I did must have become known." *(Exodus 2:11-14)* Ω

"You're fighting," Nate continues, "and like Moses, you've hit the Egyptian and offended the Hebrew. No one is listening to you. Passion doesn't matter, Ryan. That's the thing. I don't care how worked up you are, how much you want to do good work for God. It's all about what God cares about. God cares about obedience rather than sacrifice. That was King Saul's lesson. And I think that's the lesson that God was teaching Moses, too, and it's the lesson that so many of us experience, whether or not we're official pastors. God doesn't care about ordination, he cares about his people. God is working in you now more than you possibly know."

"I tried. I don't see it or feel it. Am I expected to just trust? I guess I am. That's good theology and all. But I don't know if I can. Not with all this emptiness. I feel so empty, Nate, and that's what is getting to me. What has gotten me."

"Let me tell you about Moses then. Maybe you'll see what I'm seeing. He got into his big fight. Had everything, but then lost it because he got worked up—worked up over a good thing. But his response didn't help. He was totally alone. For the first time, it seems. He had to flee. Run away from everything he knew. Forced to let go of it all."

> ▶ When Pharaoh heard of this, he tried to kill Moses, but Moses fled from Pharaoh and went to live in Midian, where he sat down by a well. Now a priest of Midian had seven daughters,

and they came to draw water and fill the troughs to water their father's flock. Some shepherds came along and drove them away, but Moses got up and came to their rescue and watered their flock.

When the girls returned to Reuel their father, he asked them, "Why have you returned so early today?"

They answered, "An Egyptian rescued us from the shepherds. He even drew water for us and watered the flock."

"And where is he?" he asked his daughters. "Why did you leave him? Invite him to have something to eat."

Moses agreed to stay with the man, who gave his daughter Zipporah to Moses in marriage. Zipporah gave birth to a son, and Moses named him Gershom, saying, "I have become an alien in a foreign land."
(Exodus 2:15-22) Ω

"Moses went from privileged son to fugitive," Nate continues. "Once again Pharaoh tried to kill him."

"Again?"

"Pharaoh gave the order to kill all Hebrew baby boys, and around that time, Moses was born."

"Right."

"All these little tidbits are important. So Pharaoh again tried to kill him. This time there was no princess to save him. Moses was a man, an adult, not a helpless baby. He chose his action and he faced the consequences. I don't know what was in Moses' head, or what was going on with God at this point. We're not told anything. Just what Moses did. We only know Moses got in big trouble. Ran away. Just when he tried to do a good work, everything collapsed. God didn't save him, it seems. Though maybe by letting Moses escape we see God's salvation. Moses had to let go of everything. And there he was. An alien in a strange land. With nothing. Where was God, Ryan?"

"I guess he was working."

"Absolutely he was working. Absolutely. Even and especially when Moses became a fugitive. Finally, Moses was becoming who God wanted him to become. But in that passage I read, we don't see that. And when we don't see the end of our own story, we get all depressed thinking we're not the same as the people in the Bible. This time, in our story, God's not going to work."

"God hasn't worked," Ryan says. "That's all I know. How can I keep going forward feeling like this?"

"What about Carrie? What about Ashley and Ethan? That seems like God's work to me."

"You know what I mean."

"I know what you mean, but I think you're wrong."

Ryan doesn't know what to do with that. And doesn't respond.

"I think you're wrong," Nate continues, "because you want to see God only in the way you want to see him. You want God to be your secret power, your good luck charm; no matter what you do he puts it right and makes it successful. You want to offer God whatever sacrifice you want to offer him and you demand that he take it."

"So what am I supposed to do, Nate? What is the right action? I have no idea what I'm supposed to do. Where am I supposed to go?"

"If you don't have an answer, that's your answer."

"Now you've gone Zen on us," Ryan laughs. "But I get what you're saying, I think."

"I'm trying to work on the art of succinctness by way of aphorisms," Nate replies and laughs. "It's true. That's what we see with Moses at least. He ran away from Egypt. Found a nice wife and had some kids. And that's it. That's it for a long time. Where was God?"

"Waiting. For some reason."

"And Moses had nothing else to do but wait. Wait while God waited. Well, maybe he could have done something else, but it seems like he became resigned. Even named his son after his circumstances. If you have another kid you should name him, 'burned out with church ministry.' I think naming kids with meaning has been out of style too long."

"I'll be sure to bring it up with Carrie. But I'm going to tell her it's your idea."

"Oh no," Nate laughs, "she already doesn't like me."

"It's not that she doesn't like you, Nate; it's more that she doesn't understand what happened." He then adds, with a wry smile, "Or maybe she doesn't like you."

They both laugh, enjoying the nice break in the tension.

"I didn't understand so much then," Nate says. "I know I didn't explain myself well to everyone and I probably said some things I wouldn't say now, even though I tried to keep it to myself."

"You did say things; that's for sure," Ryan laughs. "It took a while to get a semblance of balance back at the staff meetings."

"Yeah, I was still wanting to kill Egyptians, I suppose. But I've learned. I've learned. Always better to water the flocks."

"So how do you apply that now?" Ryan asks.

"I think, if I'm seeing this right, that Moses still acted with character where he went. He was a noble man, not just in how he was raised. He ran away but then did something right and good when he left. He didn't become a bandit or go into a life of sin. He did what was right. Who knows what he thought about God at that point, but we're told he was respectable."

"We have to water the sheep where we're at," Ryan says. "I think I get that."

"And you're getting the hang of handy aphorisms," Nate laughs.

"You're starting to get to me."

"All this to say, Ryan, I have really no idea what you should do. I'm certainly not one to tell people to stay where they feel empty or keep doing programs that aren't effective for anyone. That's why I left, you know. But I'm not you. You have that mortgage, and that's not something evil, even if it's making you feel stuck. You have Carrie and kids. All gifts from God. I didn't have that. I thought I would at this time in my life but I don't. And because of it, I'm honestly feeling a lot like you are now. So this isn't me preaching to you—I'm reminding myself of all this too. I don't know what I'm going to do either."

"So we wait? I don't know how, Nate. I don't know what that looks like. Do I just continue to play the part? Do I confess my doubts to someone?"

"Besides me?"

"To someone at the church who might make a decision for me. I don't know. I don't know what it means to wait in all of this. How do I do that?"

"You're thinking about what to do, Ryan. I don't know what to do. Yeah, maybe you should play the part. Do your job. You don't have sheep, but you do have college students. Maybe you translate all of what you're feeling in a way that is honest. I think you have to stop running though."

"Stop running?"

"You're running from Egypt still. You haven't stopped. I stopped when the Columba started coming together. Instead of trying to fix something or change the world or come up with some complex plan I just saw the people around me, and was honest with them. They were honest with me. And even if we serve beer here, this isn't the promised land. I'm still waiting for that too."

"So I should stop running." Ryan pauses for a moment, looking intently at the green awning again. "I didn't know I was running. I feel stopped. Everything looks the same. I feel like I should *start* running. Like the Egyptians are after me and will catch me if I don't get away."

"Maybe that's not the Egyptians."

"What do you mean?"

"I had to stop in order to finally be in the place where I was able to listen to God. Stop. Stop running toward all my plans."

"Stop thinking too much."

"Maybe that's it."

"I think that's what is getting me. I step back, as you're talking, and think about everything that's going on. Nothing has happened, Nate. I mean it's all in my head. My heart. But it feels so real. Like I woke up from being drugged and suddenly see the world as it is."

"Do you still believe in God?"

Ryan fidgets with his half-empty water glass, then with the knife that lies across his plate, and he pokes at the stray rice grains and chicken curry. He looks at the man and woman on the sidewalk, arm in arm, laughing together as they walk.

"Yeah," he finally answers, looking straight at Nate. "Yeah. I believe. I believe God exists. There's something still there. Someone. I just don't know what that means now: 'God exists.'" He stops, thinks about what he just said. Then adds, "There's my statement of faith."

"That's something."

"It'd be enough, Nate, if I was going into the office tomorrow to write computer code or if I was teaching high school literature. It's not enough for me to go into work tomorrow and tell kids how much God loves them and is working for them. It's not as concrete as telling them they need to put off sex and drinking and get to prayer and Bible study."

"I think you should go into work tomorrow and be yourself. Maybe you've hit a wall because you're trying to play a role. But God isn't wanting you to play a role anymore. He's wanting you to figure out who you are."

"Figure out who I am? Carrie said that you've gone New Age and that's why I shouldn't talk to you. Maybe she's right. Find myself? Like some old hippie?"

"I didn't say 'find yourself.' Like you're supposed to go off on some trek, leave behind your family and life and start eating chickpeas and melba toast. I meant really start realizing what it is you think, and hope, and want. Ryan, I've known you for what, sixteen years?"

"Something like that."

"And you've always—always—been very good about doing exactly what other people say you should do. Don't get me wrong. You are smart—way smarter than I am—and creative in what you do. You're a great pastor, but as far as I can remember you've never really shown who you are. I've never heard something that struck me as being pure Ryan Gossett."

Ryan doesn't respond for a minute, and Nate leaves his thoughts hanging there.

"You're probably right," Ryan finally responds, after moving his fork to one side of the plate and then the other, folding his napkin on the table with deliberate intent, and drinking the last little bit of melted ice from his glass. "I'm playing the game, Nate. Like you used to do. There's security in that. And I'm not just talking about paying my mortgage and paying for Ashley's schooling and all the other things that need to be paid. There's more than that. I go to these campuses. I talk with these kids. They're so young, man—so young but so old too. Older than I am in some ways. And they are fun and exciting and miserable all at once. The weight of the world is on their shoulders. Everything is open. Which sounds exciting but it's too open. Scary. The future is completely missing and they feel they have to start piecing it together. That's always in their minds. So they don't want to stop. Don't want to face that—that void. College lets them hide a while longer. But the void's there and they're crying out, crying out without having any idea of what words to use. They're crying out for someone to point the right direction, give them right counsel in whom to marry, where to work. Who to be? Yeah. Who to be. They see their parents and think they're broken and empty, but they know that unless something happens they're going to become the same person. And it scares the hell out of them. They're crying out and they're turning this way and that, seeming like they're free but they're not. They're not free at all. They're caught in all of it. They don't see a way out. There isn't a way out."

He stops; his eyes go back and forth, not looking at anything, trying to find something that he can't think of. Nate doesn't say anything. He waves off a waitress who approaches, and adds a smile when he realizes he was a little rude.

"I'm burned out, burned out with it, but I see their eyes, I hear their hearts," Ryan continues. "They're crying out. And all I can do is just keep up, try to do the things that do work, not risk trying something else that will finally end our influence all together. Keep the kids who want to listen. It's not just the mortgage. I owe these kids something. I have no idea what I have left to give, but I can't just send them on their way like nothing is wrong and go off to live my life. And that's my bind. That's why I can't just be honest and free and let happen whatever happens. These are kids' lives, Nate. Lives. Who's here if I step back and try to find myself?"

"If you can really accept this, then it will absolutely change your ministry, like it did mine. I know that sounds so Christianese, but it's so true."

"What?"

"What we learn with Moses," Nate replies.

> ▶ During that long period, the king of Egypt died. The Israelites groaned in their slavery and cried out, and their cry for help because of their slavery went up to God. God heard their groaning and he remembered his covenant with Abraham, with Isaac and with Jacob. So God looked on the Israelites and was concerned about them. *(Exodus 2:23-25)* Ω

"They cried out," Nate continues. "Their cry went up to God. He heard them and was concerned about them."

"That's Israel, Nate. That's why the Old Testament doesn't work. That's his covenant with Israel."

"For God so loved the world, Ryan—the world—that he gave his only begotten son so that whoever believes in him will not perish but will have eternal life. Have you heard that one?"

"You're saying God's covenant is with the world?"

"I'm saying that Jesus didn't die for the people we like or agree with. He didn't die for one group of people. For the world. For all of it. For everyone. So what do you think is his reaction when people are crying out for help? Ignore them? Make them someone else's responsibility?"

"Which means what for us?"

"Which means that you're thinking this is your responsibility. You're thinking like Moses did at the beginning of the story. That he felt this outrage and had to do something, anything. It wasn't wisdom, it was just frenzy. And it caused problems. He fled. He lost everything, all his authority, all his power, all his money, all his influence, all of it. He had no voice. Everything that seemed within his power to fix was gone. He did less than nothing. And fled. It all did collapse. It got worse, even."

"Right."

"But God heard the cries. Moses didn't. Moses couldn't hear them any longer. And the people never were crying to Moses. They're not crying to you now. No matter how much pressure you think you have, it's not really your problem. They don't want you, Ryan. You can't answer them. You can't even answer yourself now. But they're crying out and God hears them. He's doing the work. He's raising up people. He's working in you right now, even if you don't see it, probably more now than ever before in your life because you're finally getting to the point where you're letting go. You've stopped hitting Egyptians. It's not up to you. It never has been. This is God's mission. This is God's work, and if he's asking you to step back, or be quiet, or somehow let go, then you have to do it and trust he's hearing the cries of the people. You have to trust God now, Ryan. Really trust he has a mission stronger than you have. He has more love. More desire for people. He hears the cries. And he's doing a work, even if you can't see it or feel it now."

"I wish I could believe that, Nate. I really wish I could."

"And that's exactly what God is teaching you, Ryan. That's it. Hold on to him, and you'll get what I mean. It's his work. Not your work."

Moses wasn't being asked to have faith in Moses, he was being asked to have faith in God. God doesn't always give us answers.
He just tells us that the way forward is a way of hope.
He urges us to keep going because at the end we'll find a peace and a resolution that mere explanations will never give. He plays to win, not to justify himself.

9

when all hope is gone

Rachel Kivitz is running a little late. Her usual morning rituals got cluttered: a lost backpack, a lost wallet, a forgotten lunch. The water heater broke midway through her shower, eliciting a scream as she rinsed out her hair and was suddenly left with only cold water. Krystal, the wire-haired dachshund, decided to encourage Rachel with a gift, and didn't understand why no one seemed to value the dead finch on the couch.

In spite of all this, she is only ten minutes late, and feels no need to call. She is bothered in a vague way that's more about her instinct for being prompt and less about having someone particular to blame. Though why Mike had left his wallet underneath the towels in the laundry room she didn't know. Maybe it was the same inspiration that led Monica to put her backpack out in the garden shed sometime last evening and totally forget she did it. As Rachel gets out of the car, something else bothers her. Melissa's yard isn't right, but she can't put her finger on why. The grass is a little longer than last time, but that isn't surprising. It just seems sad in a way.

Because of her hurried morning, Rachel feels she looks like the yard—a bit sad. She had thrown on a more casual outfit than usual, left her long dark hair wet and put on an Adidas cap to cover it, rather than carefully styling it. It occurs to her this look is a lot more fitting, really, now that she's no longer an executive in an L.A. marketing firm but a full-time seminary student—spending more time with the kids and more time with God than she ever has before. Somehow, though, she's not any less tired, hence her lingering frustration and regretted words that she's hoping her daughter Monica didn't hear.

She walks up the path and tries the doorbell, then remembers it doesn't work. She knocks.

"Hey, Rachel," Tommy says after opening the door a moment later. "You're early."

"Hi, Tom. It's a quarter past nine."

"Is it? Really?"

"Yeah," Rachel laughs.

Tommy Kristoph is 5'10"—6'1" on his publicity sheets since that's what he is in certain pairs of shoes—but he seems taller than that. Something about his smile makes him irresistible; it's inviting and honest and free and daring. His green eyes flash when he smiles and talks. Those eyes and that smile are what brought him from Indiana to Hollywood, where he's almost made it for six years. His agent encourages Tom to go ahead and take children's theater roles until he finally gets plugged into the right movie role or television series. Commercials are just starting to pay the bills.

"How was the audition?" she asks.

"Pretty good. But, you know how it is—they're all pretty good. If there was an Oscar for best actor to never get an actual role I think I might be up for it. Lots of compliments. No offers. Nothing real at least. Student films aren't doing much for me anymore. That's the business though. So no complaints. Anyway, how're you?"

"I'm doing well, but my morning decided to split ways with me. We're trying to work out a reconciliation before noon hits."

"I might not be helping then."

"Why?"

"I'm supposed to pass this on: Melissa says she's sorry but she doesn't feel up to going out to breakfast this morning. It's not you, she wanted me to add, and she doesn't think she's going to be able to work on the project at all."

"What's wrong? What happened? We talked two days ago about this."

"I'm just the messenger. Though…" he looks back inside and steps out onto the porch, shutting the door quietly behind him. "I think she's hit a wall. I don't know what to do or say anymore. Ever since she went to the doctor's on Tuesday."

"I talked with her when she just got home from that. She seemed fine. She said everything was progressing. She was cheerful even. Surprised me, but I wasn't going to argue about it."

"That evening I came over and she was totally messed up," Tommy said. "I think she'd been drinking. She never drinks, so I don't know for sure, but if it was anyone else I'd say she was sloshed. I smelled alcohol. She said she had been cooking. She had made us dinner, so maybe that was it, but whatever it was, it was like she had turned off. Again."

"Like last month?"

"Worse. She barely ate. Wanted to go to bed right after dinner. I went home. I can't get her to say more than a few sentences."

"You're here."

"Because I have a key. She doesn't care if I'm here or when I go."

"So she doesn't want to see me?"

"She doesn't want to see herself, seems like. Let alone anyone else. I've got an audition this afternoon—a car commercial, but it's something—and I'm thinking I shouldn't go. I don't really trust her."

"Go. You need to go. I'll stay here."

"She told me she doesn't want to see anyone."

"Doesn't mean I have to listen. I'm tired of this, Tom. It's gone on too long. I've had a bad morning already and I'm tired of the self-pitying. I don't have the patience for it anymore. We need to talk, me and her."

"I'm not going to talk you out of it, I guess. But, for the record, could you tell her that I tried?"

"Yeah," Rachel laughs. "You were very convincing, but I am just too stubborn now that I've turned forty."

"Alright," Tom laughs. "Thanks. Don't know if it'll solve anything, but she needs you. I don't know what to say or do anymore. I've run out of ideas, besides just sitting and staring."

"Don't know if I have anything better to offer. She needs to be snapped out of this….Shoot!"

"What?"

"I really did have my hopes set on strawberry crepes and art talk. Now I have to be serious and personal and stay hungry."

"Sorry."

"I'll get over it. It's what I do. Is she still in bed?"

"Yeah. Maybe I should go in with you."

"Plead your case in person?"

"She keeps telling me to go away because she's a burden on me," Tommy explains. "Just leaving her with you might make it seem like I feel that way."

"Is she?"

"A burden? I love her, Rachel. I can't even think of it like that. Which makes it so hard. I mean, doesn't she get it?"

"No. That's the problem, I think." Rachel steps past Tom and opens the door to the small house. All the window shades are closed and it's very dark inside. The sculptures on the shelves lining the walls peek out from shadows. She continues into the hall, to the second door on her left.

"Hey," Rachel says, as she opens the door and walks into Melissa's room. "I was looking forward to hanging out all week. Mike has the kids today. You're my excuse for freedom."

"Hi, Rachel," Melissa says. She's lying on her bed, beneath a black-and-green-flowered comforter. The red painted wall across from the door has six long scrolls on it, each showing a blend of ink drawing and Chinese calligraphy. Though each scene is different, together they give off the appearance of being a panoramic view of a glade and waterfall. A slight bit of light comes through the dark, not quite sheer, jade curtains. Melissa smiles at Rachel, then looks past her at Tom who is still standing in the hall. She glares at him but hides it quickly. "I'm not really feeling like talking today, I guess."

Rachel walks over and sits on the edge of the bed. She looks back at Tom, smiles and gives the slightest wave of her head. He turns and walks out.

"How're you doing?" Rachel asks.

"I'm okay. Honest. I had a hard day yesterday at rehab—all those people—and I'm feeling tired. Getting up just wasn't in the cards for me this morning. Maybe we can reschedule? Though,

I'm thinking I'm not going to be able to help out with the installation."

"It was your idea."

"I know. But you seem to get what I was thinking about and I'm not sure I can really do what I wanted to do. Not with this." She points to her right arm.

"It takes time, Liss. We're all praying."

"It's not working. It didn't work. I'm still in a lot of pain, more than I'm telling Tom. I feel like if there was more progress—some progress—I would be able to deal, but there's not and the doctors aren't telling me much but I can see they're not exactly hopeful."

"Didn't you say it takes a long time, that's what they told you?"

"Yeah. But with what happened there's only a small chance of total recovery, and to see even *that*, I should be able to see more progress by now. Only I'm not. Less progress than before. I keep going up and then down, and I'm tired of that. I'm tired of trying to conjure up hope. I'm just tired, I guess. That's all."

"Can more surgery help?"

"Not really. Do you know the specific medical diagnosis?"

"Nothing specific."

"The bullet went into my shoulder, like you know. It caused what they call a brachial plexus injury. Meaning it damaged the bundle of nerves that connect my arm and my brain. Didn't sever them, which is good. It was the vibration from the bullet going close by, I guess, that caused the damage. Basically, it wore the nerves down really, really quickly. Or something like that. I don't really get it—my choice to be an art major instead of pre-med finally bites. So, anyway, depending on the particular injury, sometimes the nerves grow back okay. But gunshot wounds aren't those kinds of injuries. Usually. Maybe. They don't know what to expect. The initial progress made them really positive. But I hit a plateau, and maybe that's the plateau I'm going to stay at. Less pain as time goes by, but not more movement. That makes it so hard to think about anything related to art."

"It could have been so much worse," Rachel says, and puts her hand on Melissa's hand. "I know you've heard that so many times. But that doesn't mean it's not true."

"It could have been worse, or could have not happened. That's where I'm at. How do I believe in a God—omniscient, omnipresent, omnipotent, all the *omnis*—with this constantly there? Sure it could have been a lot worse. Of course. I could have died. I know that. But isn't the power of God supposed to mean something besides just avoiding the worst possible outcome? What is the power of God in this? It feels like I'm having to rationalize the lack of help in order to justify God. I don't know how I can do that. Or if I want to."

"It's a lot more than your arm, then?"

"Yes," Melissa replies as she leans up, a little awkwardly, and sits against the dark green wood headboard. "It's stuff that's probably been there all along. When I walked away from my dad's church, I had these same questions. Only then I was looking at other people and what they were going through. Now it's here, always with me, and I'm not getting past it, and I can't do what I've always done to help clear my mind. I can't pick up a brush or get my hands into some clay or pound a chisel. I sit with it. And sit with it."

"Oh, Liss," Rachel says, sitting on the bed and putting her arm around Melissa. "I don't know what to say. But I so know what you're feeling. I wish I could tell you the one thing that you need to do or just the right answer. But I don't have those.

But, honey, keep holding on—that's what I do know—because it'll clear up. You have to keep holding on. I'm here, we're here, to hold on with you."

"Hold on to what? That's what I don't know. You tell me to hold on. Deb is telling me to hold on. How can I argue with her after what she's been through? But I still don't know what I'm holding on to. She knows what to hold. You do. Tom seems to. *I* don't. I don't know how to anymore. I tried for a while, tried to act myself into believing again."

"We can't tell you, Liss, because the answer has to be *your* answer. I can't tell you who God is to you now. You've grown out of being fed. You know that, but you've only known a part of it."

"Part of what?"

"What it means to be able to face this world in faith. You're so smart. You're so beautiful. You're so talented. All your life you've been strong, even when on the inside you didn't feel strong. You've been the one to push and lead, even when people around you said you can't push and you weren't to lead. Now you're feeling lost. But nothing's changed, Liss; that's what you need to see. Nothing's changed."

"Nothing has changed? *Everything* has changed!" Melissa yells. Tears begin to flow down her cheek. "Sorry. I just need to be alone a while, I think. That's why I didn't feel up to breakfast."

"That's why I need to stay. You think you're going to drive me away? I feel like that's what you're wanting to do. Only I'm not going to go away. You can yell at me or yell at God all you want and I'm not going to push you back. You're still so amazing to me. You've been this light in my life—to me and to Mike and to everyone. You have to see that. Bringing out so much from us. Nate is great, but you've been the soul of the community. And now that the soul is hurting we're going to give back. That's what we do. No matter what."

"Thanks, Rae, and I'm sorry. But I need to hear it from God, not you. You're being nice. I appreciate that. But I need God to speak."

"Like what? From a burning bush or something? You want God to treat you like he did Moses?"

"It would be nice. At least I'd know."

"That's the thing, Liss. It still isn't enough. If you don't hold on, even God yelling at you or lighting the shrubbery on fire isn't going to help. You have to hold on in faith."

"I don't have any. Not anymore. So what do I hold on to now?"

"You know where I've come from, right?"

"Yeah."

"Well, then you know I'm not innocent or blind or anything. I've lived. Before I met Mike I lived in hell and its surrounding suburbs. For a long time. A long time. You know that, right?"

"Of course."

"I know you do. I'm asking because I really need you to know that I'm not just saying nice words. I'm really talking here, and I hope you listen. Because what I'm saying isn't just pretty words to help little Melissa feel better. It's coming from my heart and my life and it's true. I'm telling you like this because I know how strong you are. Okay?"

"I suppose."

"I know how you feel because I've felt like that too. What do you think I was feeling when I was in jail? Happy and content that all had gone well? I have a son out there I've never met except for when he was born, and I've got years and years that are gone—just totally lost because of the drugs. I'm an ex-con, Liss. Felony conviction that goes wherever I go. My past is this weight that I'll never get away from, and I've sat with the same bitterness you're feeling. No, I don't know what it's like to lose the use of my arm. But I know things you don't know and have to live with experiences you'll never, ever have to experience. I'm so sad you're sad, but when I say there's a way past it, you can't write me off. I've walked the walk, and I'm farther along than you. Okay?"

Melissa doesn't reply. She continues to stare at her curtains, a single tear making its way slowly down her left cheek.

"Can I be straight?" Rachel asks. "I feel like I need to be. You need me to be. So what I think is this: You're mad at God. You don't like him. You don't like what happened and you know, with all the faith that once gave you joy, that he could have stopped it. But he didn't. And you know why?"

Melissa turns and looks at Rachel. She has heard many attempts to answer this question and most have made her furious. Her brow furrows in expectation of her angry response.

"Why?" Melissa responds.

"I have absolutely no idea," Rachel says. "No idea at all. Not a clue. Not a hint. I wouldn't have allowed it to happen if I had the power. So we're left with theological problems, and even now with two years of seminary behind me I don't know how to answer those problems. Not really. I can give you nice words and all, but you don't want those. And I don't want to give them to you. You're past that."

"So what can you say? What's left? That I have to just deal with it?"

"Yes! Well, no. But yes! What I mean is that it's not about dealing with it, like everything is in the trash. It's learning how to live in the reality that you're in now. You think God got you into this and now you're mad he ruined everything you planned and how you planned to do it."

"Yes. Because it's true."

"And I'm not going to argue that with you."

"Are you going to tell me that God brought me through this in order to teach me something? So that I'd be better? I've heard a lot of that and it's stupid."

"Like I said, Liss, I have no idea. All I know, and I do know, is that you're not lost and you're not over, and the only one who will make it over is you."

"I just don't see a way past this, Rae. I tried. I really tried. I feel so alone. Now I'm at this point where I feel like even if God starts talking I'm too far gone to respond. It's just not in me. Not anymore."

"Honey, I know. But, I know something else too."

"What's that?"

"You're talking just like the people who God always seems to use. I joked about the burning bush, but you really are a lot like Moses."

"Deb keeps telling me I'm like Joseph."

"Yeah," Rachel laughs. "Him too. It's true. Maybe it's because we're all going through the Moses story these days in our readings, but I can't help but see you standing out there like Moses."

"Except no burning bush."

"I don't know about that, Liss. That's what's hitting me now. You don't have a plant on fire. But you're still being called by God and you're reminding me of Moses when he was called. Have you been reading with us?"

"I keep meaning to. I was going to. I open it up but the pages are blurry to me. Each word feels so heavy and empty at the same time. So I put it down again. But I know that story. We used to have a flannelgraph picture of Moses and the burning bush. 'Take off your sandals, Moses!'"

"Ha! I can hear little Liss saying that. But that's not the part I'm thinking about. I love that we're pushing to look at whole stories, and I'm really thinking there's something to it. Not looking at what I'm calling the 'publicity shots'—the kind of scenes that get made into the posters and stick with us as these great moments of God's work. And that's it with this story of the burning bush. It's a story of God reaching out after a very, very long time of silence, after Moses had been rejected and isolated. It's a story of Moses' doubt and God's persistence. Moses doubts himself, doesn't think he's up to it. Basically doesn't think God knows what he's doing. Sound familiar?"

Melissa doesn't answer but instead looks like she is restraining herself from saying something. Rachel can't quite tell if Melissa rolled her eyes the very slightest bit, but she suspects there isn't immediate acceptance of the comparison.

"Let me read this part," Rachel says. She reaches into her purse and pulls out a small red Bible. She starts turning the pages, looking for the right section. "I think it's important. God appears in the bush, and says he has heard the cries of the people. He ends with, 'So now, go. I am sending you to Pharaoh to bring my people the Israelites out of Egypt.' But it's the next part I love. God says 'go' to someone who is eager and excitable and full of ambition, and that person is supposed to answer, 'Absolutely. Where and when?' I love the way Moses actually responds."

> ▶ But Moses said to God, "Who am I, that I should go to Pharaoh and bring the Israelites out of Egypt?"

> And God said, "I will be with you. And this will be the sign to you that it is I who have sent you: When you have brought the people out of Egypt, you will worship God on this mountain." *(Exodus 3:11-12)*   Ω

"Moses doesn't say 'okay,'" Rachel continues. "He asks, 'Who am I?' This is the guy who was so full of zeal he killed an Egyptian. He was a man who felt the pain of his people. Now, after all this time—forty years or something like that—he's totally broken. 'Who am I?' He's a shepherd in an obscure part of the world. God appears to him—God!—and tells him he's the man for the job. Moses says he's not up to the job. He's broken, totally broken. His past did him in and now he doesn't care or doesn't think he's up for it. What does God say? 'I will be with you.' That's the key. That's the key to it all, Liss, don't you see? That's the word I heard when I was so depressed and thinking of suicide after that awful year in prison. That's the most important thing and that's what I think you're missing, what you're not seeing."

"That God will be with me? But he's not, Rae. That's my point. I'm not Moses. God appears and tells Moses he's with him. Great. That would clear things right up for me. But he's not doing that. Tommy was here, you're here, others. But God hasn't been, and I don't know where he is now."

"Okay, what if you aren't Moses? What if you are an Israelite still in Egypt? Where is God? Is he working? Is he listening?"

"He is with Moses."

"That's it. He tells Moses he is listening. He tells Moses he is acting. Acting on behalf of Israel. All the crap that had gone on so long isn't the end of things."

"All I feel is the emptiness, Rae. That's it. If I could muster up some kind of faith, you know I would. I hate being this person lying in her bed feeling self-pity. I hate it. I know what I would say to myself right now if I were visiting me. I would say all the encouraging words and everything else people are telling me. I know it. I know all that. But I also know that everything I thought and planned seems gone and there's no kind of comfort to make it seem okay. I just feel so empty—emptied."

"You're missing my point. Totally missing it. I'm not telling you to feel something you don't feel or to somehow muster up the 'ol' Melissa' enthusiasm. I'm not. That's not it at all. You're so like Moses, Liss. Trying to come up with more reasons. No, don't say anything. I want to read this next part because I think it helps explain what I'm getting at."

> ▶ Moses said to God, "Suppose I go to the Israelites and say to them, 'The God of your fathers has sent me to you, and they ask me, 'What is his name?' Then what shall I tell them?"
>
> God said to Moses, "I am who I am. This is what you are to say to the Israelites: 'I AM has sent me to you.'"
>
> God also said to Moses, "Say to the Israelites, 'The Lord, the God of your fathers—the God of Abraham, the God of Isaac and the God of Jacob—has sent me to you.' This is my name forever, the name by which I am to be remembered from generation to generation. *(Exodus 3:13-15)* Ω

"Moses comes up with more questions," Rachel continues. "God gives his answer. Who am I? 'I am, that's who.' God tells Moses that it's not about him. Yes, Moses is the man in front of the burning bush. But it's not about him. It's about God. It's about God. It's about God. And that's still the point. That's what you're missing now. I know this isn't nice to say, but it's true and I'm saying it because of the fact that you hit this faith crisis right when you experienced your own loss. Which means, to me, that you've based your view of God on your own strengths and abilities and dreams. You've always been talented. You've always been popular. You've always been a girl the guys would look at. You're not stuck up or arrogant or any of that. You're a wonderful, wonderful woman, Liss, but you've gotten used to being the strong one and now that you're not, now that you're not able to push yourself forward you think that it's God's failure. But I think it's something else entirely."

"What?" Melissa answers, curt and defensive.

"You're being shown it's not about you."

"So God took away my arm? Is that what you're saying to me?"

"No! My gosh, Liss, get off it. I've said that's not the case. You're wanting an excuse to get out of life because you're realizing now it's not going to look like all you wanted and planned. You're feeling weak and in need, and you hate, hate that feeling. You're dependent and you hate feeling dependent. Now that you don't know who you are anymore you're wondering where God is, because it seems so clear to you—to you and to no one else—that God can't use you if you can't paint and sculpt like you used to. You think what you loved, what you loved about yourself, is gone and now nothing can replace it. Moses was in the same place and so he kept asking questions, kept trying to come up with a reason. And you're doing that."

> ▶ Moses answered, "What if they do not believe me or listen to me and say, 'The Lord did not appear to you'?"
>
> Then the Lord said to him, "What is that in your hand?"

"A staff," he replied.

The Lord said, "Throw it on the ground."

Moses threw it on the ground and it became a snake, and he ran from it. Then the Lord said to him, "Reach out your hand and take it by the tail." So Moses reached out and took hold of the snake and it turned back into a staff in his hand. "This," said the Lord, "is so that they may believe that the Lord, the God of their fathers—the God of Abraham, the God of Isaac and the God of Jacob—has appeared to you."

Then the Lord said, "Put your hand inside your cloak." So Moses put his hand into his cloak, and when he took it out, it was leprous, like snow.

"Now put it back into your cloak," he said. So Moses put his hand back into his cloak, and when he took it out, it was restored, like the rest of his flesh.

Then the Lord said, "If they do not believe you or pay attention to the first miraculous sign, they may believe the second. But if they do not believe these two signs or listen to you, take some water from the Nile and pour it on the dry ground. The water you take from the river will become blood on the ground."

Moses said to the Lord, "O Lord, I have never been eloquent, neither in the past nor since you have spoken to your servant. I am slow of speech and tongue."

The Lord said to him, "Who gave man his mouth? Who makes him deaf or mute? Who gives him sight or makes him blind? Is it not I, the Lord? Now go; I will help you speak and will teach you what to say."
(Exodus 4:1-12) Ω

"You say you can't help out with the installation," Rachel continues. "Why? What has changed? You can't use your arm. But nobody asked you to paint or sculpt for this. We want what's inside—your creativity and insight and perspective. Who gave you those? No one has taken those away. The Spirit is still in you."

"I don't feel any of that anymore, Rae. That is what I'm trying to say. It's not that I don't want to. It's that I don't feel like I have anything to contribute right now. I don't know what to think about anything and I don't feel—-I don't *feel*, Rae. I feel so empty. What am I supposed to add? I don't care. And there's no insight coming from that."

"I'm still asking you to join in. See, that's why I am thinking of this passage. You're telling me that you don't care, that you don't have anything to say. Maybe that's true now, sitting in your dark room, but I think you have a lot, so much, to add. So much of what you've thought about and studied and done is still in there."

"But I don't know where. It feels gone. Like I've been sandblasted."

"That's what Moses felt! Here's this guy who was on top of Egyptian society. He had everything going for him. He made a mistake—had to flee, lost everything—and now he's tending the flock of his father-in-law. God says now is the time. Moses is like, wait a second I can't do this anymore! Moses is changed, so changed he doesn't have any fire left. He's not seeking to do anything. He's not looking to lead a revolution or do some kind of major work for God. He's just a shepherd now. But here's the thing. God had worked in the past by saving Moses and that wasn't wasted work. God did a work for a reason and it doesn't matter if Moses felt it in that moment. It was God's work. Fully and totally—what God did in the past was being activated in the present for a work in the future."

"That sounds like a seminary phrase," Melissa says, with a faint smile. Two tears slowly make their way down her cheek.

"I have to impress you with my intellect and education somehow," Rachel laughs. "That's the key to being a good pastor. Watch me pull out some Greek in a moment, so you'll listen without arguing."

"If I didn't argue then it'd be a sure sign I'm totally lost."

"Well, keep arguing then," Rachel laughs. "I can't tell you to ignore what has happened to you or to dismiss it. I can't give you any answers for why it happened. But I know that this isn't all that happened. We don't know why you were attacked. We do know that God has worked in your life—through your life—in so many ways in the past. He gave you such creative gifts, such a sharp mind and strong, wonderful personality. So much integrity. I'm always amazed how you are so intent on being you. God has worked, Liss. In you and through you. So what you're doing now isn't just saying that your arm is messing everything up for the future. You're saying that all God has done has been lost because there's nothing else. You're saying God's work in the past can't lead you to a fruitful future because you're so, so caught up in what's happening in the present. You're saying God can't work and you're challenging him like Moses did."

"What can I say if I don't have anything to say, Rae? What can I possibly do? I don't know how to work or live like this."

"You've got questions now and I'm trying to tell you that God is saying he's going to work it out, that you have to trust him for your future. Trust that he has called you and he's not going to let you go just because evil got its hit."

"Rae, I don't know who I am anymore, not with this," Melissa says and points to her right arm, lifting it ever so slightly, a grimace on her face with the effort.

"That's what Moses is saying, Liss. Moses was done too. He had left that identity behind him and now God shows up and Moses is so broken, so far away from his old self, that he actually starts arguing with God, bringing up one question after another, thinking that maybe God hasn't thought this through."

"But God's not talking to me through a burning bush. That's my whole point. I get that God can work but he's not giving me this call, he's not telling me that he's going to do these miracles to prove himself. I'm not an atheist. I know God exists. I am just really thinking he doesn't exist *for me*. Where is he? Moses had him right there. I wouldn't argue with him if he were right there. I'd take my shoes off and I'd listen. It's a fact that everything I thought I heard when I was really going strong now seems to be meaningless. Maybe I'm just not one of the elect. I'm not one of those chosen by God. So he's not really working in my life. Do you get that?"

"What am I?"

"What do you mean?"

"Am I some random woman who likes to go to people's houses and bring artificial cheer so that I can feel good about myself?"

"No."

"I walk with God, Liss. I do. I spent a long time away from him, living in hell and totally alone. But I'm not there now. I walk with God and we chat. The Holy Spirit is in me. I can say that with absolute assurance. The Holy Spirit is in me. So why would God light the flora on fire now? He did then because he was so hidden. Now? He has his people—people he has put into your life to speak to you just as you speak to us. So you want to hear God's encouragement, that God is going to continue to work in your life? *I* am telling you right now that's exactly the way it is. Moses didn't want to believe it when the bush was talking. You don't want to believe it now when I'm talking. You want to hold onto your questions because they are the last gasp of all your dreams. Now, though, there's something different going on. I can't say what. I have no idea. But I know, because here in Exodus and all through the Bible, we see that God calls and works, even and especially after we think the dreams are done. He tells us to go forward—that's the message—even if all our questions aren't answered."

"How can I go forward if I feel so empty by what has happened? I'm not trying to come up with excuses, Rae. I would love to have this great vision of the future. I hate—I absolutely hate—feeling like a loser. I hate it, but it's what I'm feeling. It's what I see now. It's there and I'm not going to play a game—your game or anyone else's game—pretending that I am totally great. That's why I need to come to terms with this. And I don't even know how to come to terms with it. I don't know where to look because everyone is telling me, "just have faith" when that's precisely my problem, and it gets in the way of everything; I just don't have faith anymore. And I wonder now if I ever did, or if all along I was playing a game because being spiritual was a helpful part of what I wanted to do. I'm going to keep asking questions. That's where I'm at, and if you don't see that but instead want to lay out again all the Christian crap I've heard all my life—which hasn't given any answers—then I'm not sure there's any more to be said. I'm sorry I can't help out with the installation. I'm sorry I'm in this situation. I'm sorry I can't play the game anymore. But that's how it is right now."

Rachel stares at Melissa for a few moments. Twice she begins to say something, but each time pulls back before any words get out. Melissa stares back, not saying anything else, though clearly ready to challenge a potential response. Rachel stands up, straightens her blouse, takes off her cap, and runs her hand through her hair. Melissa watches as Rachel walks over to the window, opens the curtain a very little bit and looks out at the side yard where a row of roses, planted by Melissa's grandmother, grow untended and unkempt. The roses don't seem to mind, however, and bloom white and red and prize-winning pink. After about thirty seconds Rachel closes the curtain, tighter than before, blocking even the little sliver of light the morning sun is so eager to offer. She stands staring at the jade green curtains and then picks up her purse off the vanity and begins to walk out. At the doorway of Melissa's bedroom she stops and turns back toward the bed.

"At the end of that conversation," Rachel says, "you'd think that Moses would have been content. He asked his questions and he got answers. God responded to him."

"Rachel, I don't..."

"No, let me say this. Let me finish. You think I'm just like your family or old church friends? You know who I am and then accuse me of just trying to play the Christian game to avoid questions? I don't even know what to say to that, it makes me so mad. You've lived this easy life—easier than so many people I've met—and now you're hitting a rough patch and think you're the only one who has troubles. That's fine. Wallow in it, Melissa. Be who you want to be, okay. But let me finish what I have to say because I think I've earned the right to speak."

Melissa doesn't say anything.

"God responded to Moses after all the questions, but when Moses got his answers, he figures they aren't enough. He tells God, 'Please send someone else to do it.' He tells God that he's not up to it. He's broken and ruined. That's his identity now. What does God say? 'There, there Moses, I'll keep answering everything until you're convinced? No! God got mad. Because God was saying go, and Moses was saying no. Nothing could fix it. There weren't any answers. There was just faith. Moses wasn't being asked to have faith in Moses, he was being asked to have faith in God. You want to wallow in this, Melissa, that's fine. You want pity; you want to let your attack define you. Go ahead. But you know where I'd be if I let all my past and all my unanswered questions bog me down and keep me from hope and new life? I'd be miserable. Maybe even dead. Now I've found this life, a life I never expected or knew to hope for. Because I walked forward. I trusted when God said go. I didn't let my guilt or absolutely stupid past whisper darkness into my soul. That's what God is asking. He doesn't give us answers, Liss. Sometimes he does, but not always. He just tells us that the way forward is a way of hope. He urges us to keep going because at the end, in his way, we'll find a peace and a resolution that mere explanations will never give. He plays to win, not to justify himself. And I want to win. I want to win with him. So I keep walking. And I hope, I pray, you keep walking with us. But it's up to you. No one can make you."

Rachel turns around and walks into the living room and out the front door. Five minutes later, Melissa hears a car start and drive away.

And we know that in all things God works for the good of those who love him, who have been called according to his purpose.

(Romans 8:28)

10

when God calls

"So, how is everyone tonight?" Nate asks.

A dozen or so men and women are gathered around the large table in the back room of the Columba Pub and Restaurant. It's Wednesday evening and now finally cooling off after a long, hot day. The open windows and front door provide a welcome breeze.

They've spent the last hour talking with each other over salads, drinks, and dishes of various kinds. Most everyone knows each other, and already knows how the others are doing. A few people Nate knows only because they became regulars at the Columba and then became intrigued with the conversations going on around them. He doesn't think they are Christians, but he figures it's the Spirit's job to nail down those details. He's just going to do his part and share his thoughts as they come, hoping something resonates.

"Exodus 4 this week," Nate says, standing up at his chair. "Moses has been given the job, but now he's interviewing God. 'Um, what's your name?' Little twist on the normal process. Terrible interview overall, really. Moses points out all the gaps in his resume and brings up his weakest qualities himself—his real weakest qualities, not the 'I sometimes work too hard and hope too much' kind of weaknesses. It's a fun chapter for me because it shows, I think, how God chooses who he will choose. I'm at this point where I'm wondering what I'm supposed to do next, and that comes with probably too much self-analysis, not all of it positive. Reading this was hard, because I like to ask the questions like Moses did. Hard, but good for me because it put the focus squarely back where it should be—back on God. I've probably been thinking too much about me, and not about God, and so of course I feel the weight of it all." He sits down. "So, that's my extensive, scholarly laden overview for your edification. Let's talk."

The conversation begins slowly, like it usually does on these evenings. Nate occasionally asks a question but much of the time silence does the trick. Sit still long enough and people open up and respond. The wait staff clears the plates, leaving only glasses of assorted shapes on the table, and more than a few cups of coffee and tea. The group talks about Moses' conversation with God, noticing how oddly reluctant Moses seems only a few chapters after seeming the total opposite—a hotheaded, murderer.

Rachel sits on the far side across from Nate, not saying much. He's not surprised. She's the kind of person who rarely speaks, but listens intently all along, and then, occasionally, offers an unusually insightful comment. Nate has stepped away from pushing the conversation because of this. He sees Rachel as one of the two people who might take more leadership responsibilities when he leaves, but he hasn't told anyone that. As he's not entirely sure who the second person might be, it seems likely he'll have that conversation with her soon. Maybe include Mike in further talks. Fortunately, Rachel is also one of those people great at saying no—which makes Nate even more eager to have her step up. He's also aware that she may feel content with what she's doing.

"This first part really hit me this week," Rachel says, breaking a lull in the conversation. Nate looks over at her, a little surprised. "I had a breakfast meeting scheduled with Melissa and it came up."

"How's she doing?" Nate asks.

"Up and down. She had some bad news this week about her progress—I'll let her share the details—and was feeling discouraged. I had just read through this first part the evening before and it was fresh in my mind. I think that was God's work because the words here just filled me up and got my blood going. Something just hit me about what Melissa was saying and it was like this passage suddenly became totally clear to me."

"What was clear?" Amanda Lopez asks. Amanda arrived late to the meeting but everyone understood. The traffic coming from Los Angeles is always worse than expected, and it's always expected to be bad. She is extremely well-dressed—quite fashionable—which surprises a couple of the first-timers who had only seen her at the Sunday-evening gathering where she explores the ranges of casual with passion. She just turned thirty-five, and as a birthday present—what she calls it at least—her advertising company promoted her to account supervisor. Her plan is to work for a few more years in her present job, saving money along the way, and then start working for nonprofits, using her training for people who don't often have access to high-end advertising expertise. She hasn't told her boss about this, of course, and is still open to wherever God leads her.

"Something we've talked about before," Rachel answers, "It's all about God. That's where I think I've put so much wrong stress on my life. When I started seminary it was the end of a really long struggle. 'Who am I?' I asked myself. For years. I remember even when I was young—like twenty—thinking how amazing it would be to be able to just study God. I had so many questions. But I knew my life, and knew I wasn't the kind of person God wanted, or anyone else wanted. That dream lingered, and popped back at the weirdest moments, but I was always like, 'I'm not good enough.' And I kept getting worse. I mean at twenty I was still relatively innocent. I had a talk with Melissa, telling her my thoughts about what God was doing, and when I walked out to the car afterward, it hit me how much God had been talking to me all those years too. Only I kept ignoring him, kept writing him off, dismissing those whispers—whispers of the Spirit, I guess. It was God calling. God calling me to step up and learn about him and maybe teach about him to others who didn't know where to go or how to listen or what to think because of all the distortions out there—all those people who say they're speaking for God but don't have a clue to what he's really saying."

"What is it he's saying?" Karl asks.

"Different things, Karl. Different things to different people. But I think what is true is that he's saying 'I am' to all of us. God is calling, talking to us, and he's the one with the power to do what he will have us do. I thought it was about me. And I was so, so, so wrong and lost so many years."

"Maybe you didn't lose those years," Lisa says. "Maybe they were part of God's work too."

"Maybe," Rachel replies. "Not that he led me to that, but that he uses those times, that wilderness time."

"Makes me think that Moses kind of got a taste of what was coming up," Karl says.

"What do you mean?" Nate asks.

"I mean that it seems like Moses is the one complaining here. I don't mean to jump ahead of the story but I can't help think that Moses is talking like the Israelites later talk. He's had his time in the wilderness. He's doubted God's work. And he's here arguing and complaining and saying, 'Leave me alone.' And

God gets mad at him and works anyhow. It's like the later story in microcosm."

"That's like what it says in Second Corinthians," Chris Patterson adds. Chris is the manager of the Columba Pub and Restaurant, during the day at least. He's average height, with shoulder-length dirty blond hair, and a tendency toward maintaining eye contact a bit too strongly, a trait that has led to a variety of retail-management and restaurant-management positions over the years. "Here it is," he says, after flipping through his Bible.

> ▶ "Praise be to the God and Father of our Lord Jesus Christ, the Father of compassion and the God of all comfort, who comforts us in all our troubles, so that we can comfort those in any trouble with the comfort we ourselves have received from God. For just as the sufferings of Christ flow over into our lives, so also through Christ our comfort overflows. If we are distressed, it is for your comfort and salvation; if we are comforted, it is for your comfort, which produces in you patient endurance of the same sufferings we suffer." *(2 Corinthians 1:3-6)* Ω

"I know that's not exactly the same," Chris continues. "But maybe that's like what Nate has been saying. Paul is talking about consoling in affliction. Maybe this isn't just about that, but about teaching, or leading, or whatever. He puts us through situations that we are later supposed to help others through."

"I'm not sure I want to say 'God puts us through' these things, Chris," Rachel says. "I know what you're saying, but I think it's good to be more precise here with our words. Because there's so much hurt caused and so much distortion when we talk about God *causing* the evil. I do think you're right. Those are perfect verses because they aren't saying that God is causing the affliction. It's God causing the *consolation*, and that consolation we pass on to others, however that looks in each situation. Sometimes consolation means giving a hug and sometimes it means using challenging words to get a person up and moving. That's what I like about this conversation with Moses. God is gentle with Moses at the beginning. But by the end he gets mad, tells him how it is."

"Not because God is rejecting Moses," Nate says. "We see anger and think it's rejection. But God isn't doing that. Jesus didn't do that either. Jesus got mad at his disciples. Not because he was rejecting them like he was so many religious leaders. He was calling them. It's because God is calling Moses, calling us, there's consolation."

"We need to be snapped out of our distortions; that's right," Rachel says. "I got kind of frustrated with Melissa, I have to say, and now I wonder where I was with that. With God's consolation or my own impatience?"

"What did Melissa say, Rachel?" Amanda asks.

"Oh, I'll let her talk about it if she decides she wants to," Rachel responds. "But with all she's dealing with, she's feeling like she has lost her part. Only for her it's so sudden. Others—myself, certainly—took a long time to get to the place where we felt emptied and so it wasn't as dramatic when we began to believe all the distortions. I like what you said, Karl. Because I think that's true. Moses got a taste of what was coming up. He had the situation Israel had—favor, brokenness, and restoration—only it was within his own life."

There's a long lull. Rachel takes the last piece of garlic bread, breaks it in half and hands one half to Debbie who sits next to her.

"So what else comes to mind about this passage?" Nate asks, after a short pause.

He looks around the table. A few folks stare back in waiting expectation. Most everyone looks away, taking a drink of water or fidgeting in the chairs. No one says anything.

"I read this," Luis finally says, "and it hits me how much God isn't limited to our understanding of time. Moses is arguing with God, and finally says 'no.' But before that, before there was even a conversation between God and Moses, God had already nudged Aaron. Let me read this section again, because I want to know what you think about it."

> ▶ But Moses said to the Lord, "O my Lord, I have never been eloquent, neither in the past nor even now that you have spoken to your servant; but I am slow of speech and slow of tongue." Then the Lord said to him, "Who gives speech to mortals? Who makes them mute or deaf, seeing or blind? Is it not I, the Lord? Now go, and I will be with your mouth and teach you what you are to speak." But he said, "O my Lord, please send someone else." Then the anger of the Lord was kindled against Moses and he said, "What of your brother Aaron the Levite? I know that he can speak fluently; even now he is coming out to meet you, and when he sees you his heart will be glad. You shall speak to him and put the words in his mouth; and I will be with your mouth and with his mouth, and will teach you what you shall do. He indeed shall speak for you to the people; he shall serve as a mouth for you, and you shall serve as God for him. Take in your hand this staff, with which you shall perform the signs." *(Exodus 4:10-17 NRSV)* Ω

"Seems to me," Luis says, "that God is working. He's working even if we don't know it and even if we don't even care anymore. He's working in ways we don't know and so our part is just to listen to what we're being asked to do." Luis is not a big man, but he seems it to most people. There's a strength in his eyes, a piercing, yet kind look that seems to know more than he actually should. Not surprising given his work as a psychologist; people feel exposed around him. His dark hair and skin is contrasted by the light gray polo shirt and tan Dockers he has on, as well as by what he feels is a disconcerting amount of white in his hair. His wife, Natasha, says the white in his hair makes him look distinguished.

"Jeremiah 29:11," Karl says, "'For I know the plans I have for you,' declares the Lord, 'plans to prosper you and not to harm you, plans to give you hope and a future.'"

"Exactly," Luis says. "Just because he knows the plans doesn't mean he shares them with us right away."

"Can I ask a hard question?" Prisca says. She is one of the few who have joined in even though they aren't part of the regular community. A few weeks before, she shared that she went to church when she was young—up to high school—but hadn't been since then, making it about fifteen years or so. She never said why she stopped going, even though she has been fairly open in conversations. Well, open to a point. She includes herself but mostly listens, and doesn't volunteer too much besides the fact she's curious about spiritual things and that she spent most of her twenties going to—as she put it—'too many and too wild' parties. She's a little shorter than average, a little rounder than average, and she laughs a lot, often more as a filler than as a response.

"Of course," Nate replies. "Hard questions are the best kind of questions."

"How do we know when God is working and when we're just alone and nothing is happening? I think you're saying Aaron was already being sent. But sometimes there's no Aaron and there's just—well—nothing. We're kind of left on our own. Have you ever felt that? Do you get what I'm asking?"

"It's not about having the same kind of answer that we see here," Luis answers. "But it's more that God is working, already working, to help build what we need. We're not left alone, or left isolated, even when we think we are. Even when we have given up. God knows not only our strengths—why he calls us—he knows our weaknesses and makes up for those. But not necessarily in the way we like. He's pushing us farther. Moses here really just wanted to be left alone. He didn't have what it takes; so he thought. But God was working, not only asking. He was telling Moses to go, and undermined Moses' excuses, even though going would still be a huge amount of work. He's asking us to go, even though we don't see the support yet. But it's there. He's laying tracks even as the train is moving along. We look ahead and get worried because there are no rails. But he's laying them down as we go, just when we need to run over them to keep going. If we stop, or turn, or whatever, that's when we get derailed. Aaron was on his way. God had already been laying down tracks even though Moses hadn't seen them yet."

Amanda jumps in, "God doesn't give the power until we need it. That's so true with what I've seen. And I've missed him, missed those moments of God's work because I let my doubt get in the way. God seems to send an Aaron to us when we need support. Maybe it's not our well-spoken older brother or something else clear. Maybe it's just an opportunity, a conversation, something that is perfectly timed. If we do our part and participate with God, we can become a tremendous blessing. If we let our fear get in the way, the blessing doesn't happen. God told Moses to keep at it. And he did. Even though he said no, he followed up, with a little help from big brother."

"Like the parable Jesus told, about the son who said 'no' but did it anyway," Mike adds.

"Yes," Amanda says.

"I like that, Amanda," Nate says. "Moses is going. He might not like it. But God is convincing here. Moses doesn't respond to his fears; instead he steps out."

"I like that he admitted his fears," Prisca said. "That's important; something I'm learning how to do."

"We're not honest with ourselves," Luis says, "and so don't even recognize when God is honest with us, what he's done, how he's moving."

"We don't know where to look," Rachel adds.

"It's like a do-over in a way," Debbie says. She has been sitting at the end of the table listening. Her shift ended only about ten minutes before the gathering started, and she is feeling a little too tired to be here, but she doesn't let that get in the way.

"What do you mean?" Nate asks.

"We see him at the beginning," Debbie continues. "He kills the Egyptian. Totally impulsive. Just acts. Doesn't consult or involve anyone. Expects them to respond. They respond differently than he expects and suddenly he's left totally alone. He runs away. Totally broken up. Has this new life. God gave him a passion, but it wasn't worked out right. Moses messed up. God called him back, but this time he was supposed to do it right. Include others, follow God—maybe we could say he was supposed to hear the Spirit."

"Moses is back," Karl says with dramatic flair, mimicking the popular movie-preview announcer's deep voice. "And this time he's brought God with him."

"And not just God," Nate says. "God pushed Moses to seek *others*. Moses didn't go alone. He didn't just show up and tell everyone how it was going to be. Even though he was so clearly working under God's guidance, he went through a process of getting others on board; he joined with God in that. First they got Moses' father-in-law involved."

> Then Moses went back to Jethro his father-in-law and said to him, "Let me go back to my own people in Egypt to see if any of them are still alive."
>
> Jethro said, "Go, and I wish you well."
>
> Now the Lord had said to Moses in Midian, "Go back to Egypt, for all the men who wanted to kill you are dead." So Moses took his wife and sons, put them on a donkey and started back to Egypt. And he took the staff of God in his hand. *(Exodus 4:18-20)* Ω

"Then they brought Aaron into the picture," Nate continues.

> The Lord said to Aaron, "Go into the desert to meet Moses." So he met Moses at the mountain of God and kissed him. Then Moses told Aaron everything the Lord had sent him to say, and also about all the miraculous signs he had commanded him to perform.
> *(Exodus 4:27-28)* Ω

"So what does this say about what God is doing in Moses?" Nate asks. "I want to add that I'm not pushing for a specific answer, trying to lead people. I'm genuinely curious."

"If it's God's work among people," Chris says. "Then God doesn't just tell one person, right? I saw that at the church I grew up in. The pastor there had a vision, he said, for the church. Whenever people disagreed or had questions, he questioned their devotion to God. People who persisted were asked to leave. Whole families left. My family left after a number of years of being really supportive of the church and the pastor. If there was conflict or disagreement the pastor would put on his religious, pious face and then say how he had prayed about this very issue and God told him what people were supposed to do. And that generally meant giving him more money or more power."

"That's convenient," Deb says.

"For him," Chris replies. "That's for sure. But it wasn't really. There was such turnover there until he finally had surrounded himself with people who parroted what he said and did. Just the sort of people he wanted to lead. Only they were also the kind of people who were really dysfunctional. They wanted approval, not Jesus. They wouldn't have said that, or maybe they didn't even know that, but that pastor was caught in this trap of wanting creative, inspirational, teachable people and yet passive, immature, and gullible people at the same time. He cut out people who had been there for years and years and brought in new people. All because he thought it was his role to tell people, to decide for them. But people disagreed, and he continued to assume that he was the one God was talking through. To them. Not among them, or with them."

"So there's this confirmation we're seeing," Nate says. "God works for communities, among communities, not through only one person."

"Even if there's one person who takes a leading role in something," Luis says.

"That's it," Nate responds. "God might have one or a few people do particular things that he doesn't necessarily also ask others to do. But that one person or small group of people are still asked to find agreement with people who are seeking God too—people who will be affected by their actions."

"I remember when I was young," Amanda says. "There were always these boys around—good Christian boys from good homes—who were so into studying the Bible and praying and really seeking God. They talked about their future in missions or doing God's work in the marketplace or nice things like that. Not insincere at all—not most of them. In high school and at the small Christian college I went to, I seemed to attract these boys like flies. They'd ask me out, and we'd go to dinner or whatever; I was terrible at turning boys down then, sometimes going out because I felt sad for them and wanted to reward them for their courage for asking. Then, again and again, whether after just that first date or a couple, they would write me or sometimes even tell me face-to-face that they felt God was calling us to be together. So they'd be instantly in this serious relationship with me, even though I was just looking for an evening out. They'd say, 'God made us for each other' or something, and I'd be somehow polite in answering but inside I was, like, 'Um, no. God didn't tell me that and I'm sure he'd fill me in too.' They wanted to impose some kind of spiritual authority on what was going on in their pants. It became funny after a while."

"That's not just for young guys, Amanda," Deb says. "They don't grow out of it. A guy I kind of knew through mutual friends came up to me at a party about eight months after my Courtney died—I think the first party I went to—and told me that God told him he was supposed to—I love this—'fill the void' and take care of me from then on."

"What did you say?" Amanda asks.

"I don't even remember," Deb replies. "I'm usually quick with comebacks but that totally knocked me back. I wanted to hit him, and kick him. My whole being, everything in me was saying, 'No! No! No!' to this ass. Maybe that's harsh. He was kind of a weird guy and I don't think he was ever intentionally offensive. But when I thought about it later I realized how I wasn't just reacting to him, but also to the genuinely evil men who were around me growing up, who used religious language to satisfy their grossness and who manipulated people left and right with their supposed authority—destroying lives. It took me years to separate those men from the man they claimed to represent. They were antichrists, I know. Nothing about them was right but they put all their words into pretty packages and pious smiles....Sorry to get on that tangent."

"No, I think that totally adds to what we're talking about," Amanda says. "People who don't learn how to listen with God—to include others—are on the wrong path. They might start off innocent and sincere. But they can get trapped in that and become real enemies of God."

"Like the Pharisees were with Jesus," Karl says.

"That's it," Nate says. "What was Jesus' issue with them? They had separated the law from God and the people. They made religion into their own thing, not God's thing. And Jesus blasted them. Because God's work is a community work."

"There's also the humility involved, and I think that makes a difference," Luis adds.

"Moses had to get permission," Prisca says. "To act for Israel, I mean."

"Something like that," Luis responds. "Here's a guy who had everything. He was saved from his own disaster early on, but still wasn't one of the people. He had gotten out of the neighborhood, so to speak. People figured he forgot where he came from, and when he tried to show how much he cared, he found out that he was a man without an identity. He couldn't force himself into either one, no matter what he did. Trying to be a savior—someone who reaches down from the lofty heights—made him even more suspect. Who did he think he was?"

"By this chapter—nobody," Nate says.

"That's it, Nate," Luis says. "By this time he really was a nobody. An alien in a strange land doing work no one else would do. He had lost it all, but he was still the guy God wanted. And there's this really godly humility we see here. It's not the depression or self-deprecation we saw earlier in chapter 4. That's not real humility; that's faithlessness—telling God that he can't work through you or me. But now Moses has been brought through the wilderness to discover real humility, and that means trusting God is working while at the same time trusting that God isn't working only through him—just as it means trusting God isn't working only through you or me. So, we're drawn into this community of God's work, where we have to let go of both our ambitions and our frustrations."

"You're reminding me," Nate says, "of something I read the other day, and wrote down in my Moleskine." He reaches into his bag and pulls out a small black notebook, and opens it. "Here it is: 'Those engaged in spiritual warfare can escape from the cycle of trial and temptation only by recognizing their weakness, and regarding themselves as strangers to righteousness and unworthy of any solace, honor, or repose.'* We're being taught, like Moses was, to learn how to handle our own pride and temptations and ambitions and frustrations."

"Are you saying God brings disasters to us in order to teach us?" Rachel asks, a questioning look on her face.

"That's a hard question, Rachel," Nate replies. "Because there's not a single answer. Sometimes yes. I have to say that because it seems God pushes us through hard times so that we find maturity. But not every symptom has the same root cause. Sometimes I think God allows us trials for our sharpening. Sometimes bad stuff just happens, and there's no getting around the fact that it's evil. But even that stuff isn't left without God's stamp on it, if we are able to keep the faith going through it. This is what I see when I read Romans 8:28."

---

* *Nikitas Stithatos*, The Philokalia: The Complete Text, *trans.* G. E. H. Palmer, Philip Sherrard, and Kallistos Ware, vol. 4 (London: Faber and Faber, 1995), 113.

"Now there's an overused verse," Deb says.

"Yeah, it is," Nate replies. "And used so often as a cliché. But let me read it, read it now as we're talking about Moses' humility and now his seeming restoration."

> ▶ And we know that in all things God works for the good of those who love him, who have been called according to his purpose. For those God foreknew he also predestined to be conformed to the likeness of his Son, that he might be the firstborn among many brothers. And those he predestined, he also called; those he called, he also justified; those he justified, he also glorified.
> (Romans 8:28-30)   Ω

"Far from being just a nice little cliché encouragement for people going through problems, there's this profound point here that Paul is making that I think I missed for most of my life."

"Because people leave out verses 29 and 30," Rachel says.

"I think that's it. Those are the interpretive keys for us. We usually define *good* according to what makes us happy. We think that good equals *living the good life*."

"Our territories will always enlarge," Karl adds, with a sarcastic chuckle.

"People interpret that according to their own desires and wants," Nate says. "Which often means making us less dependent on others, or making us in charge of others. It often means us having power and authority and wealth, so that we're set free from people bothering us."

"If people stop bothering us," Mike says, "and if we don't have to ask them what they think, then we can really get to the 'good work of doing ministry;' because they listen to us, and they do what we tell them to do. We try to make it so we aren't constrained by their lack of faith."

"What we *call* their lack of faith," Rachel says to her husband.

"Right, we confuse their lack of faith in us with a lack of faith in God. When in fact if we really were walking with God, God would be giving everyone the same message, like Amanda mentioned."

"And God's goal," Nate says, "is sometimes different from our own."

"To conform us to the likeness of his Son," Deb says.

"We're all made in the image of God," Nate says. "But we're not like him anymore. All the junk gets in the way. Not only sin, but our lack of perspective, our ambitions. Stuff that sometimes even puts us in conflict with God."

"Sometimes, it's conflict with God even when we're thinking we're doing God's work," Mike says.

"Can I clarify this?" Prisca asks. "This is all new to me and I want to see if I'm hearing right. I hope I don't sound stupid."

"Please," Nate says. "You definitely don't sound stupid by asking. We're all exploring this together."

"God is not telling us he's going to be giving us what we want, right? But that he's doing this bigger work, that he's shaping us to be better people?" Prisca asks.

"Not just for us, though," Luis says. "Become better people for the sake of everyone. Becoming good neighbors, really. I like what you're saying, Nate, because it gets at what I think is so lost in our era. We lose sight that God's goal is to bring total victory, not just a nice present for us. God is about this bigger thing—making us whole—and working in the process of bringing real freedom. But it takes humility and faith to walk with God in this, because we only see the small stuff. So we don't always trust God to walk with us. Which is why he works to shape us to trust him."

"To dance with him," Rachel says. "This makes me think of the Holy Spirit in our own lives."

"How so?" Nate asks.

"Well, there's that verse that talks about grieving the Spirit. It seems to me that the Spirit invites us to join—invites us to choose to walk with God's plan."

"Like Moses was invited," Nate says.

"Like everyone in the story was invited," Rachel replies. "Aaron was invited too. Jethro was asked for his blessing. We're asked."

"Can we say no?" Prisca asks.

Rachel pauses for a moment. "Yeah. Yeah, I think we can. I mean, maybe, it seems to me. God presses us, but he doesn't force us. If we're too caught up in other stuff we can get distracted, and end up wandering."

"Makes me think," Karl says. "I wonder if maybe God called young Moses to help bring relief to the people—not as a foreign shepherd but as a prince of Egypt."

"I was thinking that too, Karl." Deb says. "I mean, who's to say? We're certainly not told, but it seems like that would fit. God asks, but doesn't make us. Maybe Moses got a feel for the call, but was too immature to go the way God asked. He got impulsive and took matters into his own hands. Forced the issue, and everything got screwed up, so he went into his own wilderness for a while."

"But if we do it with God," Nate says, "we do it together and we do it in a way that draws everyone out of the wilderness, into this shared worship of God. That's how chapter 4 ends."

> ▶ Moses and Aaron brought together all the elders of the Israelites, and Aaron told them everything the Lord had said to Moses. He also performed the signs before the people, and they believed. And when they heard that the Lord was concerned about them and had seen their misery, they bowed down and worshiped. (Exodus 4:29-31) Ω

"Contrast that to Exodus 2," Nate continues, "where Moses does his own thing, tries to be the hero, and ends up being an exile. People aren't helped. God is not glorified. Moses tried to fight the evil, and got crushed. Here God is asking him to do something relatively easy. How are the people going to be freed according to the new plan?"

"Moses is going to ask Pharaoh to free them," Jen answers. Jen Hoeffler is the administrative assistant for the community. Jen was born in Los Angeles, near the house by the University of Southern California where her grandfather was born—an old turn-of-the century home where just about every weekend her extended family still gathers for good cooking. Most of them at least. Her brother got shot the year before; died on the operating table. Wrong place, wrong time, between the wrong two people. It's been hard for her to go back ever since, even harder recently, for some reason.

"That's it, Jen," Nate replies, with enthusiasm. "God tells Moses just to ask—to show up and ask. God is going to show his power and do the rest. When Moses takes this proposal to the leaders of Israel they see that it's not about Moses and him being a hero, but about God and God answering prayers."

"It seems hard—this added suffering along the way," Mike says. "But I know from my own life that sometimes it's so much easier to put the walls up; try to block that stuff out."

After a short pause, Mike begins talking again. "When I lost my church, lost everything, I thought that was the end, that God hated me. Even though I knew it was my own fault, I still wondered where God was—where his grace was. The first place I saw God's grace was his not letting me do more damage to people because of my very encouraged and very empowered immaturity. God broke me down. And then he put me together again. I lost command and leadership and the appearance of wisdom. But I found out how to follow God's plans, not doing it myself to fit what I thought were his goals. I found out how to be truly right with God before all of it. To make prayer not an afterthought but the only thought. I found that I'm not supposed to impose on people—found that out in battling with Nate a little bit."

Mike pauses momentarily. "And I found you all, found real community and real acceptance and real wisdom that's not about us doing some mission and fighting for God. Instead it's about peace and hope and being in this real relationship with God. That's what he wants from us, that's what he wants with everyone."

"That's it," Nate says. "We get distracted so easily, and then lose heart or lose purpose or lose perspective. But God is really wanting us. Really wanting us to be whole and participating with him. He wants real and thorough and humble obedience where we really are in this together, not just with each other but all together with him."

"I want that too," Prisca says.

Moses returned to the Lord and said, "O Lord, why have you brought trouble upon this people? Is this why you sent me? Ever since I went to Pharaoh to speak in your name, he has brought trouble upon this people, and you have not rescued your people at all."

(Exodus 5:22-23)

11

when it's one step forward and two steps back

The day is a little warmer than the day before; the early afternoon breeze brings with it overtones of winter, cool and crisp. Sweater weather. The sun is out and working, heating up the bench on which Debbie and Rachel sit. The coffee cups in their hands help even more, warming their hands while the hot beverages they sip warm them on the inside. Birds sing spritely tunes, suggestions of spring. All around remain signs of last night's storm: Broken branches cover the wet grass; dark spots remain on the shady patches of sidewalk.

"I really don't know what to say to her anymore," Rachel says. "I realize I probably shouldn't go over today because I'll just be mad; I've let it get the best of me. I mean, I want to see Melissa, and probably even should. But I shouldn't. Know what I mean?"

"If you could do it right, it'd be nice," Debbie responds.

"That's it. But I know myself enough now to see that I'm likely not able to do that. My buttons have been pushed. I guess it's a good thing to be reminded that I'm still immature in some areas." Rachel takes a sip of her coffee and then laughs. "God is good at doing that with me."

"Yeah," Debbie laughs. "I'm reminded a lot of that too."

"Reminded how immature I am?" Rachel asks with a mock seriousness.

"No!" Debbie laughs. "Reminded how immature *I* am sometimes. However," Debbie continues as she puts her hand on Rachel's shoulder, "God has pointed out a few things that he wants me to share with you about how you can do better."

"I'm sure he has. I think I'll need a new legal pad to take down all those."

"Maybe a couple," Debbie laughs, then turns serious. "Personally, with Melissa, I'm on the other side of things. I'm totally okay visiting. I was there last evening. But I'm feeling like I should say, or do, more than I'm doing. I can see her loss of faith, but I can't bring myself to push at it more. I feel like I'm missing my responsibility somehow by not giving her the 'seven steps to complete spiritual recovery' or something like that. Or at least giving her just the right book so some wise writer can say it perfectly so she sees the light."

The screech of tires and brakes, then intense honking grabs their attention. A car at the nearby intersection got confused by the light for the turning lanes and started into the intersection, right in front of a line of cars turning from the other direction. The driver doesn't seem to know what to do while the honking continues and the cars begin to swerve in front of him. After sitting in the middle of the traffic a few more moments, the car finally backs into the crosswalk. Debbie and Rachel look at each other, wide-eyed.

"That's what I'm talking about," Rachel says and laughs.

"Love the handy illustrations you work out," Deb responds.

They watch the chaos move back to order, and Rachel says, "This stuff with Melissa has made me think about all that has gone in my life. How God worked, I mean. I think that's why I'm so frustrated. And not at Melissa; not really."

Deb stares at Rachel with a crooked smile.

"Well, maybe a little at Melissa," Rachel admits, laughing. "But a lot of it is with me. I think back to how God worked to bring me out of all that mess, and I feel it so deeply but I can't put it into words."

"You could just tell her what you can. You've helped me understand."

"I try to talk to her. But it's not the same."

"Like Pharaoh didn't see it either," Deb says. "Even with a lot more than words."

"Yeah, that's true. Kept getting hit with the plagues but it wasn't ever enough."

Debbie doesn't respond right away but instead takes another long sip of her coffee and watches the two finches, one with a bright red head, jumping from branch to branch in the tree across from her. There's a squirrel with a thin tail higher up. She just notices him up there, sitting on his haunches eating something, looking quite happy with his find.

"I'm still thinking about your question," Deb finally says. "About what happened with me. And about Pharaoh and the plagues and stuff. It's funny how as we're studying this I just keep seeing more and more—in my own life, I mean."

"I am seeing that too," Rachel says. "I get what Nate has been trying to say. About there being a pattern. We're in this story, aren't we?"

"And I guess that's hard to explain to someone who doesn't see it from the other side. I see that now, you see that now, but Melissa doesn't see it because it just seems like everything is getting worse, and so she's angry at us for trying to give her hope."

"She's angry with God," Rachel says. "That's who she's angry with. We're just convenient."

"Yeah, she is, but she's angry with us too. I can see that. Maybe she doesn't want to be and she's not playing it out, but I see it, especially when I've made the mistake of saying something spiritual or trying to be hopeful. She gets really defensive then, and it's not about God. When I'm around her I feel like I'm a fake, even when I know in my deepest heart I'm saying what I know to be true."

"Maybe that's part of it," Rachel says. "I guess that's what we see in Exodus, too, though. Moses finally goes to Pharaoh, in chapter 5. But it doesn't help. Moses and Aaron do a big show for the Israelites, explaining God's plan. They get everyone on board. But then, when they goes to Pharaoh to claim the victory, Pharaoh laughs at them, kicks them out, and makes everything worse."

"I haven't read yet this week. That's chapter 5?" Debbie pulls a small yellow Bible out of her handbag and turns to Exodus 5. A robin flies into the tree above them and begins singing.

"A little chorus with our reading," Rachel laughs.

"Meeting in the park is a great idea," Debbie says. "I spend so much time in the pub these days. Burns me out on everything."

"I need to get outdoors," Rachel replies, "Out into a piece of God's world. I want to take advantage of it more."

"Here it is. Should I read the whole chapter?"

"Yeah," Rachel replies. "I'd like to hear it again after what we talked about."

> Afterward Moses and Aaron went to Pharaoh and said, "This is what the Lord, the God of Israel, says: 'Let my people go, so that they may hold a festival to me in the desert.'
>
> "Pharaoh said, "Who is the Lord, that I should obey him and let Israel go? I do not know the Lord and I will not let Israel go."
>
> Then they said, "The God of the Hebrews has met with us. Now let us take a three-day journey into the desert to offer sacrifices to the Lord our God, or he may strike us with plagues or with the sword."
>
> But the king of Egypt said, "Moses and Aaron, why are you taking the people away from their labor? Get back to your work!" Then Pharaoh said, "Look, the people of the land are now numerous, and you are stopping them from working."
>
> That same day Pharaoh gave this order to the slave drivers and foremen in charge of the people: "You are no longer to supply the people with straw for making bricks; let them go and gather their own straw. But require them to make the same number of bricks as before; don't reduce the quota. They are lazy; that is why they are crying out, 'Let us go and sacrifice to our God.' Make the work harder for the men so that they keep working and pay no attention to lies."
>
> Then the slave drivers and the foremen went out and said to the people, "This is what Pharaoh says: 'I will not give you any more straw. Go and get your own straw wherever you can find it, but your work will not be reduced at all.'" So the people scattered all over Egypt to

gather stubble to use for straw. The slave drivers kept pressing them, saying, "Complete the work required of you for each day, just as when you had straw." The Israelite foremen appointed by Pharaoh's slave drivers were beaten and were asked, "Why didn't you meet your quota of bricks yesterday or today, as before?"

Then the Israelite foremen went and appealed to Pharaoh: "Why have you treated your servants this way? Your servants are given no straw, yet we are told, 'Make bricks!' Your servants are being beaten, but the fault is with your own people."

Pharaoh said, "Lazy, that's what you are—lazy! That is why you keep saying, 'Let us go and sacrifice to the Lord.' Now get to work. You will not be given any straw, yet you must produce your full quota of bricks."

The Israelite foremen realized they were in trouble when they were told, "You are not to reduce the number of bricks required of you for each day." When they left Pharaoh, they found Moses and Aaron waiting to meet them, and they said, "May the Lord look upon you and judge you! You have made us a stench to Pharaoh and his officials and have put a sword in their hand to kill us."
(Exodus 5:1-21) Ω

"Stop there," Rachel says. "This is it. This is what's in Melissa's soul right now. We always go on in the reading but so many people spend years and years stopped right here."

"We know the end already of this story, so we just want to get to it."

"And we never trust God is working in the middle of our story. But he's telling us this story so we know our own story.

We're given hope. We're told there's something more. Then life turns bad and we get even more angry than before. At least we had hope before, but after that even our hope is gone."

"We like nice order, I think," Debbie says. "We want things to be bad, and then be good. No gray areas. I hate gray areas because it's not one or the other."

"There's transition. We forget the transition, and the yanking and pulling and letting go and tearing apart that often comes with it. I mean, I get what Melissa is feeling. She had dreams and now she doesn't know how to dream those dreams anymore, and those dreams were what propelled her all the way along. She got robbed and shot—who gets *shot*?—and yet she still had that Melissa courage for so long. We prayed. Everyone gathered together. She had doubts at first but then when she got out of the hospital she was a rock of faith. Encouraging everyone else."

"Because she saw all the progress," Debbie says.

"She had hope in how the story was *supposed* to go. She didn't need to have it all solved right away because she knew the stories of God's work. Something bad happens. People pray. Boom! It gets better. That's the story."

"That's how even this story is told. I still remember from Sunday school Mrs. Kennick teaching us about Moses and Pharaoh and how the people were brought out of Egypt. We went from the burning bush to Aaron coming to visit, then right to the plagues, talking about how God worked so miraculously. It was all about the miracles—the plagues, Charlton Heston with his arms stretched over the Red Sea, the manna. All the good stuff."

"And that's what it is, isn't it, Deb? It's really a faith thing. We might still appreciate God but we don't think he can get us out of whatever problem is right in front of us. When things don't get better, and then get even worse, it's like our whole soul deflates."

"What's interesting to me—and I've never thought about it like this before—" Deb says, "is their response. Moses goes to Pharaoh—finally he's convinced and does what God asks him to do—and then Pharaoh responds with total arrogance. Dismisses God. I mean why would the slaves' god deserve respect, right? Pharaoh strikes back; shows everyone who's boss. He's not defying Moses, he's defying God, right to God's face. The Israelites get the brunt. They get mad. But who do they get mad at? This is what gets me right now, because it makes so much sense."

"They get mad at Moses," Rachel answers.

"Exactly. They even call God's judgment down on him, when Moses is the one who has been following God's commands. But they get mad at Moses because they can't admit they don't have faith in God. Basically, they agree with Pharaoh. And they can't direct their anger in the right direction. So they start lashing out at who is convenient, who they can point to as being the apparent cause for their problem. That's huge; that's so, so much of what I see in my life. I couldn't get mad at God, but I was so, so mad at him all my life because of what he seemed to allow. He didn't defend me, Rachel. I mean he was there—I never doubted he was there, even when I was hiding from the men, the leeches—but he didn't stop them. Not until I ran away and got myself out of there. I don't understand that. I still don't. But I couldn't be mad at God—I wouldn't let myself. So I was mad—raging—at everyone else, and I added so much more chaos to my life because I didn't know what to do. So I got so mad at the church, at pastors. I was so mad with everyone for so long that it's a miracle I'm here talking like this."

"I'm so with you on that," Rachel says again. That's me. That's exactly me. Well, not the reason for the anger, but I had the same whole lot of anger at God I didn't know what to do with. So I know we blame anyone else who seems connected. Because we want them to be the problem."

"It brings in more and more chaos."

"It's like a fix or getting drunk. Helps us not to think about the problems, but it's bad in the long term."

"That's right," Rachel laughs. "I never thought of it like that. Bad Bible interpretation is like getting a fix. People get lost in it for years and never grow up."

"But unlike users, they feel all justified and important. Anger and pride go hand in hand. At least drugs bring humility."

"Sure do," Rachel says. "Again and again and again. Feeding back into itself. What do we do? That's the question and that's the only one we can answer. We can respond the right way or we can respond the wrong way."

"I came face-to-face with this after Courtney died. I certainly can't blame God for all the messes I made, but I blamed him for making things worse and not helping me when I needed it. I mean, I didn't blame him consciously, but looking back that was at the heart of how I reacted."

"Choose faith. That's the essence of it. Choose what is right in the moment. We cause so much chaos because we're not able to admit our lack of faith or our anger or anything. We just don't know how to be honest so we throw everyone else in the fire to hide the stench of it."

"Which is what Israel is doing here," Debbie says.

"Exactly. Moses does what God asks. He goes to Pharaoh. All hell breaks loose. Everything gets harder, because there's this huge battle when the chains are being loosened. They chafe because they are starting to get loose. The Israelite leaders totally accepted that Moses was sent by God. They gave him their blessing. But then when things turned bad they turned against Moses, and did so with false piety. 'May the Lord look upon you and judge you,' they said. Calling down God onto Moses."

"Which was basically calling God to judge God," Debbie adds.

"Yeah, they deflect it and go on the attack," Rachel says. "The church I was at before this one did that all the time. I was getting my life back on track, totally on fire and committed to God, and loved how dedicated they were to the Lord and to the Scriptures. At first I loved their vision and mission. It drew me in. But there was never any input allowed. I started learning more and studying more and getting more into the Word myself. I was leading a small group—that's where I met Mike, by the way—and was involved in leadership. I listened as again and again they attacked the people in the congregation. Not to their faces, but behind the scenes—always blaming one person or another when they weren't stepping up. They saw every setback or deficiency as a sign of our consumerism or lack of faith or something. They never looked at their own selves, or adapted their vision to what people were saying. They blamed the people who were trying to just find light there. They refused to blame God for not bringing in the thousand people or the finances for the new building project or any of the other plans they had. They kept up their piety while always blaming others, totally alienating people."

"That's why I like Job so much," Debbie says. "Because his life has everything going wrong—everything—but he doesn't blame anyone else."

"Not even himself."

"Not even himself," Debbie laughs. "That's right. He puts the problem right where it is. With God. He goes straight to God. Won't let anyone distract him. There's boldness and humility in that. Which I think God respects. I think God wants us to be mad at him if that's what we're feeling. He wants our emotion and our thoughts. He wants us to look the right direction."

"God got mad at Job's friends."

"They were like what you're talking about—" Debbie says, "trying to find a reason, trying to justify God. God totally shot back at Job, but he respected him, it seems. Meanwhile God totally blasted Job's friends. That's been huge to me."

"That false sense of what is religiously 'proper' is totally destructive," Rachel says. "I think that gets Israel too. They get mad at Moses. But Moses doesn't get mad back at them. He doesn't misdirect his anger. He goes right to God, brings their complaints to the source they should have gone to. And God gives Moses encouragement."

"God understands us a lot better than we understand him. I like that. He's willing to meet us where we're at."

"But he doesn't let us linger there."

"No," Debbie laughs. "He absolutely doesn't. He is always pushing us, trying to move us forward, trying to get us out of our Egypt. But he knows how to deal with us where we are, in what we need."

"We still get confused," Rachel says. "But that's okay too. Moses takes the question to God—just like Job did. Moses didn't understand either, but finally he had faith. He had been broken but he knew for a fact God had called him and he brought that to God. God was being insulted by Pharaoh."

"And the Israelites, really," Debbie adds.

"Yes, he was being insulted on both sides. So Moses asks what's up. We can do that. We can always ask and seek counsel and comfort—even if we don't get the answer to the *why* question."

"Okay, here's the end of chapter 5." Debbie begins reading:

> ▶ Moses returned to the Lord and said,
> "O Lord, why have you brought trouble upon
> this people? Is this why you sent me? Ever

since I went to Pharaoh to speak in your name, he has brought trouble upon this people, and you have not rescued your people at all."

Then the Lord said to Moses, "Now you will see what I will do to Pharaoh: Because of my mighty hand he will let them go; because of my mighty hand he will drive them out of his country."

God also said to Moses, "I am the Lord. I appeared to Abraham, to Isaac and to Jacob as God Almighty, but by my name the Lord I did not make myself known to them. I also established my covenant with them to give them the land of Canaan, where they lived as aliens. Moreover, I have heard the groaning of the Israelites, whom the Egyptians are enslaving, and I have remembered my covenant.

"Therefore, say to the Israelites: 'I am the Lord, and I will bring you out from under the yoke of the Egyptians. I will free you from being slaves to them, and I will redeem you with an outstretched arm and with mighty acts of judgment. I will take you as my own people, and I will be your God. Then you will know that I am the Lord your God, who brought you out from under the yoke of the Egyptians. And I will bring you to the land I swore with uplifted hand to give to Abraham, to Isaac and to Jacob. I will give it to you as a possession. I am the Lord.'"

Moses reported this to the Israelites, but they did not listen to him because of their discouragement and cruel bondage.
(Exodus 5:22—6:9) Ω

"That is interesting," Debbie says, looking up from her Bible. "Moses asks why. I didn't see that before. Moses asks the question we all want answered, in this story and in our own lives. But God doesn't answer it. He doesn't answer why."

"He didn't answer Job's question of why either," Rachel says.

"No, he didn't," Debbie replies after a moment's thought. "He basically answered Job with a 'who are you to ask me' response, even though God seems to have liked that Job pushed the questions. Why is that, do you think?"

"I don't know."

"I sort of think it's because even though we ask why, that's not really what we want. What we want is an answer—an answer to the problem. Understanding why sometimes seems like an answer; even if things aren't better we can at least know why they were bad in the first place and maybe try harder or do something more."

"God doesn't say *why* because he goes straight to the heart of it," Rachel adds.

"Yeah, he says what he is going to do about it. He's the strong, silent type. Doesn't waste his words."

"I've always liked that type."

"And then you married Mike?"

"Yeah," Rachel laughs. "The chatty, fastidious type."

They both laugh at this. Rachel takes another sip of her coffee, tips it way back and scrunches her face as she realizes it's cold now. She gets up and asks Debbie if she's done with her coffee too. Debbie hands her the cup and Rachel walks over to the trash can about fifty feet away. When she turns around to go back, Debbie is walking toward her.

"We've been sitting for a while," she says. "Let's stroll."

"Alright," Rachel laughs, then looks back at the bench.

"Here you go," Debbie says, and hands Rachel her purse. They walk along the curving, concrete path as they get back to talking.

"What is also interesting," Debbie says, "is that Exodus doesn't say the people were wicked or stupid or whatever."

"Stiff-necked," Rachel adds.

"Yeah, I like that one. Stiff-necked and stubborn like we're told later. Here they're really in the midst of hell. God's plan for their deliverance has been set in motion, but they're not on their way out of Egypt yet. They're feeling the weight of their bondage more than ever. But God understands. The despair and the discouragement—all of it. Their feelings come through—they're not whitewashed."

"Let me read the end of that passage," Rachel stops walking and pulls out a small pocket Bible from her purse. "I like God's response here. The people don't believe Moses, and Moses goes back to God and tells God the people don't believe him. God doesn't get into a discussion about how to convince them. Here it is."

> ▶ Then the Lord said to Moses, "Go, tell Pharaoh king of Egypt to let the Israelites go out of his country."
>
> But Moses said to the Lord, "If the Israelites will not listen to me, why would Pharaoh listen to me, since I speak with faltering lips?" *(Exodus 6:10-12)* Ω

"God doesn't even respond to the Israelite doubt," Rachel says. "He goes right to the heart of the matter."

"What does God say to Moses after this?" Debbie asks as they start walking again.

"He tells Moses how it's going to go down."

"How it's going to 'go down'? You're so cute when you're trying to be hip," Debbie laughs.

"I try," Rachel laughs in response. "It keeps me young. Anyway, God tells Moses that Pharaoh won't listen. But that doesn't matter."

"Pharaoh doesn't have to believe Moses, because God is going to be the one doing the convincing."

"That's it," Rachel replies. "It doesn't matter. God is going to work anyhow. Moses is the one who had to have faith and just do his part in being the messenger."

"Seems like he quickly forgot about Aaron," Debbie says. "And remembered his excuses. He's discouraged too, it seems."

"But he just has to do what is in front of him. That's the key! Nothing more than that. And not worry about the outcome. God is going to take care of it all, in his timing. He plays to win."

"I like that. God plays to win. That's really it, isn't it? We have to keep that in mind."

They walk in silence for a moment.

"So why don't you think Pharaoh listened?" Debbie asks, "I mean do you think it was his choice, or was it—as you put it—the way God had it go down?"

"Are we all street now?" Rachel laughs. "No, I think he had a choice. Or maybe God knew what choice Pharaoh was going to make, because he knew Pharaoh's heart."

"Doesn't it say somewhere that God made Pharaoh's heart hard?"

"It does say that," Rachel replies. "I think I get that now, though, from how God worked in my life. Or get it in a way that makes sense to me."

"What do you think?"

"I had this friend, Anna." Rachel says. "Beautiful girl. Total party girl too. Then something happened. She 'caught religion' we said. And she totally did, but not in a judgmental way. She was just happy. None of us were happy even though we thought we were doing things that were supposed to be about enjoying life. Then Anna and I were together, at some family thing—she's my second cousin—and happened to sit near each other and I asked her what was different. She told me. She so told me. Said I just had to let go of all the crap and there's peace to be found for me, too, with God. I was so lost then. I didn't want to let go of any of that. Didn't want to listen at all. I look back on that now and see that's when I really started going downhill. Isn't that weird? Life wasn't great but it was okay and I was surviving. Then I got into dealing and my life became an absolute mess."

"How is this like Pharaoh?"

"Pharaoh was totally caught in his lifestyle. Everyone bowed down to him. He was happy, I think, or he thought so. Everything was easy and going well, and here was this guy coming and telling him to make major changes, to basically upset the social order as he knew it. Coming in with this talk about another god and this god's demands for a slave people. Who would want to be involved with slaves, right?"

"Who would want to be involved with religious people?"

"That's it!" Rachel replies. "Religious people look like slaves, don't they? Don't party or get high or anything. But that's the lie right there. Anna saw freedom—that Romans 8 freedom—and I couldn't recognize it. She was there, telling me about this new way, and I totally rejected her. I think God was giving me a chance then. But because I hardened my own heart I wasn't ready for it—God had me wander a while longer. Not because he hated me, but because I wasn't going to listen to him as I was; I couldn't listen. My heart was hard and so I went for a long time thinking I was still on top of things, only to find myself absolutely at the bottom."

"God takes his freedom seriously," Debbie says. "Don't mess with God when he's offering freedom or when he's telling us to give someone else freedom."

"He takes freedom so, so seriously. Exactly. Exactly. I was causing chaos, not seeking freedom."

"Here's my car," Debbie says, standing in front of her blue Honda Civic. "Thanks for the talk. I don't know what to do with Melissa, but I'm getting a better feel for the whole situation. For my situation, I guess."

"Me too. That's why we meet up for these talks. I think we have to somehow convince Melissa that she has to have hope in God, that he's still working, even when things seem to be worse. Actually, I think this is God's mission with her, not ours."

"That makes it easier for us," Debbie says. "Though it's hard to let go of the responsibility."

"We can only do what we can do," Rachel says. "I'll talk to you later." She gives Debbie a big hug. Then she walks down the sidewalk back toward her apartment.

In you, O Lord, I have taken refuge; let me never be put to shame. Rescue me and deliver me in your righteousness; turn your ear to me and save me.

(Psalm 71:1-2)

12

when you can't see a way out

One of the staff members had propped open the door, making for easy access to the two bookshelves of used and discounted books that Book Trails Coffee and Bookstore keeps outside. The day is perfectly fine—one of those days that makes people forget exactly why they don't like living in Southern California. A few scattered, puffy clouds hang in the brilliant blue sky. A light breeze brings gentle relief from the warmth of the sun, but isn't enough to cause people to worry about hats or loose paper.

Larry Nguyen rolls his wheelchair through the open door and up to the coffee counter. The barista sees him coming and starts making Larry's usual order—a twelve-ounce mocha. They talk a little bit about the band, Fontucky, that had played at the coffee shop the last weekend. The concert was a bit unusual for most of the regulars—country not being entirely popular in this urban area. But the band was both good enough and inviting enough to break through the audience's initial reluctance. Larry even bought a CD, thinking their song "Living the 909" might have a good chance to become a hit. The barista doesn't agree with his prediction, but Larry plans to mention the band to his cousin, who's a fan of that kind of music.

With his mocha in hand and the conversation winding down, Larry rolls past the tall bookshelves to his usual table—the one with the best view of the intersection. People on their way somewhere. People crossing paths, and sometimes crossing purposes. These realities intrigue him. The alternating politeness and rudeness reveal much more about human character than the particular humans themselves would ever admit. Watching the intersection, simply absorbing the action, was more relaxing for him than just about anything else. It was almost hypnotic, really. As he watches, analogies reveal themselves—contrasts and comparisons evolve into ideas for his work. And more often than not, those ideas unknot the tangled thoughts that push on his mind—the intertwining thought strands that come from being both a college professor and a community activist.

Larry turns the corner and notices a woman sitting at his favorite table. He tries to gauge how long she might be there—there are no signs of longstanding occupation such as a computer or notebooks, and the coffee cup in front of her did seem to be rather light when she picked it up, and tilted far when she drank from it. He realizes he knows her. She's facing away from him so he can't be sure, but then the sling on her arm confirms it.

"Hey, Melissa," he says, rolling up to the table. "Mind if I join you?"

"Hey, Larry," Melissa answers with feigned cheer. "Sure thing. I'm not going to be here much longer, though. Just on my way out. Places to go. People to see."

"You seem happy," Larry says as he moves the chair off to the side in order to wheel his own chair up to the table. He takes a sip of his mocha. Just a small sip. It's still too hot.

"Trying to be," she replies.

"How's the therapy coming along? I remember my therapy. Brutal at first, but they know what they're doing. It helped."

"Not doing too well, for me," she replies. "I'm supposed to be there now, in fact. This is the second one in a row I've skipped."

"Why?" Larry asks, a strong note of concern in his voice.

"What's the point?" she answers. "My arm isn't going to work right anyhow, so a little here and there isn't going to make a big difference. I'm tired of obsessing about it, Larry. It's all I've thought about now for months. I can't go back to before the shooting, right? So, I have to live with what is, and find a way to not be constantly angry and sad about it. That means I need to let go. People keep telling me I need to do that, and so I finally have listened."

"I don't think they meant stop going to therapy," Larry says.

"I know, and I'm probably going to get some grief about it. But it's how I'm applying it. It seems right and fine to me. I need to focus my fight in other directions. Finding how to live. Live with what I have now and what I *can* do."

"It's not an either/or thing," Larry says, his voice taking on the tone he usually reserves for his classroom. "You don't know how much difference it will make. There are always stories of doctors being shocked by recovery."

"They weren't shocked with you," she replies, then instantly regrets saying that. "I'm sorry, Larry. That was mean and wrong to say."

"It's true, though," Larry replies. "My legs didn't recover. I guess I'm not a great success story in that regard. But that's neither here nor there. I am so glad I kept at it, because even though it didn't work out, at least I knew. I knew I did what I could. It was good for my mind and my heart."

"Your heart?"

"My willpower, I mean," he replies. "It was a transition for me. And you haven't had that yet."

"That's what I'm doing now. I'm transitioning. All my life I thought of myself as a burgeoning artist. Never really discovered and certainly never rich. But hopeful. And I just about tasted it the last few months. So close, right? That door shut. So, there must be something different for me. I can't keep pushing against a closed door, right? Everyone has been praying, and this is where I'm at. Letting go of all pretense of being an artist, so that I can do something productive with my life finally, like my dad always wanted. He was right, I think."

"You sound less like you're letting go and more like you're resigned to your fate."

"Maybe," she says. "Probably. Is there a difference?"

"Absolutely," Larry replies. "Absolutely. I mean, I'm going to be the first in line to encourage people to do something practical, but I don't hear you talking about a change that is coming out of your passion. It's coming out of your resignation. That's not exactly transforming."

"I'm fine, Larry," she says. "Really. Better than I've been in a long time."

"Because you're accepting your slavery, finally?"

"What?"

"You're telling me the chains aren't so bad now?"

"That's not it."

"Look, I know how tiresome it is. I know the storms you're in—and the storms you've come through. I get that. I lived with that." He stops abruptly, and then continues. "I'm sorry. I'm getting on my own soapbox here. I'm not your counselor. I'm just your friend who cares about you."

"No, it's okay. I mean, I don't want to hear a lecture, but...."

"I only lecture when I get paid," he laughs. "I think you're just dealing with something close to home. I want to make you see how I see. Save you some trouble, maybe. That's all."

"I don't get to use my 'you don't understand' card with you," Melissa adds, with a soft laugh.

"You could try, but it won't get much traction," Larry replies. "But you do have your own story and it is different from mine. So, I don't pretend to get all that you're specifically facing. But I have faced the loss of goals and hopes and comfort. It's the comfort stuff that I realized I missed."

"My painting was always such a stress relief. Ever since I was little."

"That's what I'm talking about. We lose not only the big stuff but the things we didn't even realize we needed. Distractions. Amusements. Freedom. I used to always be at the beach, ever since I was young. Boogie boarding, surfing, volleyball, whatever."

"You lived near the beach? I never knew that. Which beach?"

"My parents owned a small restaurant in Costa Mesa. I helped out there, made some money, and otherwise was at the beach."

"What about school?"

"That's what my parents always asked," Larry laughs. "School wasn't interesting. I put in an appearance when I had to."

"You were twenty, right? When the accident...."

"Yeah, twenty. Had my new Kawasaki out on the 55. Car changed lanes without looking. I was going...going too fast. Swerved, spilled, and that was it for me. Don't remember much for a few days after that. Funny how I remember so perfectly each moment up to hitting the ground. The driver looking back, too late, his hair neatly combed. Weird, I notice the hair. Lost it all in a moment. Everything I knew. And that's what I'm talking about."

"I'm not following."

"Suddenly, I was thrust into the wilderness. Into nothing I knew. I didn't even know myself then. My identity was caught up in what I was doing. Fun stuff, yeah. But I don't know who I was with that. It was a slavery because I was caught, lulled, by it."

"So the accident freed you?" Melissa asks. Her mouth tightens. She stares right at him.

"That's a hard question, because there's not a quick answer. Yes and no. I'm a better person now, more fulfilled. But it wasn't freeing. I wasn't just one person then another. There was wilderness, and it was very hard. Very hard. People try to be encouraging and say how things will work out. But they don't mention the details. The tearing, the frustrations, the fears. Having to spend a long time mourning what we lost, what we will never have. That's why you have to walk with the process you have and not stop."

"You're trying to get into my mind now," she laughs.

"No, just trying to say how I've felt this story weave into my consciousness."

"You better just tell me what you think. Philosophy is over my head these days."

"It's what I do," Larry laughs. "That's why they pay me the big bucks." He pulls a book from the bag hanging behind him and opens it up. "Makes me think of what we talked about this last week. We did the plagues. That's always exciting stuff."

"We're going from philosophy to the plagues?" Melissa asks. "I'm not sure that's an improvement."

"Nate suggested we each look at a specific plague, sit with it for the week, then come back and talk." Larry's mind is on the Bible study and Melissa's comment barely registers. "Interesting perspectives—everyone contributed something different, even the folks who had the same plague." He laughs after realizing the unintended joke. "Anyway, talking now reminded me of something." He continues to turn pages. "Here it is," he continues. "Exodus 14. You mind?"

"Go ahead," Melissa says, then glances at her watch, and then out the window.

Larry catches her inadvertent show of impatience, but carries on.

> ▶ When the king of Egypt was told that the people had fled, Pharaoh and his officials changed their minds about them and said, "What have we done? We have let the Israelites go and have lost their services!" So he had his chariot made ready and took his army with him. He took six hundred of the best chariots, along with all the other chariots of Egypt, with officers over all of them. The Lord hardened the heart of Pharaoh king of Egypt, so that he pursued the Israelites, who were marching out boldly. The Egyptians—all Pharaoh's horses and chariots, horsemen and troops—pursued the Israelites and overtook them as they

> camped by the sea near Pi Hahiroth, opposite Baal Zephon.
>
> As Pharaoh approached, the Israelites looked up, and there were the Egyptians, marching after them. They were terrified and cried out to the Lord. They said to Moses, "Was it because there were no graves in Egypt that you brought us to the desert to die? What have you done to us by bringing us out of Egypt? Didn't we say to you in Egypt, 'Leave us alone; let us serve the Egyptians'? It would have been better for us to serve the Egyptians than to die in the desert!" *(Exodus 14:5-12)* Ω

"'Leave us alone,' they said," Larry repeats. "'Let us serve the Egyptians.' Which makes sense. They weren't as free as they thought they were and that makes for panic. Happens all the time. That's why so many societies stay trapped in political oppression, by the way. It takes so much to be able to not respond to everything as it comes crashing down. And it was definitely crashing here."

"Would Pharaoh have killed them?" Melissa asks. "If he caught them, I mean?"

"Maybe not. But he was asserting his power over life and death, and that's terrifying. They forget in a moment what they didn't like and they want the old life back. Better to serve than to die. That's the motto of broken people throughout history."

"I get that. But I don't get how this applies to me. I mean you say you were trapped, lulled as you put it. You see your past. I wasn't like that. I liked me. I knew me. I wasn't trapped. That's the point. I was already free, free from what I saw as the trap of the church I grew up in. I was doing what I loved, what others loved me doing...."

"You want it to make sense, to all connect in a logical way."

"That's exactly it. My life, my past, my situation. Where's the fit with me and the story people keep telling me to look at?"

"I don't know, Melissa. That's my answer. I don't know. I don't know what is in your heart or your mind, or what you're dealing with inside. I don't know what God is doing specifically in your life. I can't tie this together in a neat little package topped with a cute bow. I don't know where you have been with yourself or God. I just know it only works to keep pushing on with the faith. Like Moses said when he answered the Israelites."

> ▶ Moses answered the people, "Do not be afraid. Stand firm and you will see the deliverance the Lord will bring you today. The Egyptians you see today you will never see again. The Lord will fight for you; you need only to be still."
> *(Exodus 14:13-14)* Ω

"That's it to me," Larry says. "That's what you have to remember. When I was in the hospital my mom left me a Bible. Didn't say anything—she wasn't much of a speech giver—and just put it on the nightstand. Took me a week to open it. I turned to Psalms and read. Got to Psalm 71. Everything changed with that. It gave me a tool. A place to stand. Not understand, mind you, just to stand."

"What's Psalm 71 say?"

"Just the first two verses."

> ▶ In you, O Lord, I have taken refuge; let me never be put to shame.
>
> Rescue me and deliver me in your righteousness; turn your ear to me and save me.
> *(Psalm 71:1-2)* Ω

"I had a faith," Larry continues. "More like a set of statements I would say I believed in, if asked. But it wasn't really my own. Didn't make a difference to me. Lying in that bed, though, it was all or nothing. I had a choice right there. I had a prayer to pray. Something I could pray, that didn't demand too much of me but said everything. Of course, first I had to choose to take refuge with God or not. I did. My life has never been the same. But see, that doesn't mean there wasn't a whole lot of pain and struggle after that. Like here with Moses. He says what he says, but there's still that water in front of them and a raging army behind them. He doesn't say don't be afraid because of what God has done; he says don't be afraid because of what God will do. We keep our eyes and hearts on the future, Melissa."

"That's what I'm trying to do."

"Maybe," he replies, with a sigh. He takes a sip of his drink. "Maybe not."

"What?"

"I think you're standing at the back of the Israelite crowd and turning toward the Egyptians with open arms, saying, 'I, for one, welcome the return of our Egyptian overlords.'"

Melissa doesn't know what to say.

"You're capitulating, Melissa. You're not striving after freedom. You're embracing your attack as defining you. You've gone Vichy on us."

"Vichy? What's that?"

"Not just what. Also who. It was the name of the government of France during World War II. Well, the government that existed under Nazi occupation. Charles de Gaulle was the leader of the French Resistance who would not accept the Nazis as rulers of France. Philippe Pétain was a World War I French war hero who saved France from the German armies then. But after the defeat of France early in the second World War, he basically capitulated saying that the way to French existence was with, rather than against, the Nazis. He became an authoritarian ruler and punished those who disputed the Germans. Instead of fighting forward, he turned around and basically said the way forward was to give up the French identity. After the war he was tried for treason and sentenced to death, though that was commuted to life in prison. Basically, he had no faith. His Vichy government was an attempt to embrace the slavery and call it the future. And that's what you're doing. You've lost faith in what you're called to do so you're trying to embrace some old slavery, calling that your new purpose. But it's going backward, Melissa, and even though you were such a hero to us all, I'm not sure I like what you're representing now. It's not courage."

Melissa is silent. She looks around, her eyes not focusing on anything as she gathers a response.

"Sorry to be so blunt," Larry says. "I just call it as I see it. Probably too blunt. You're tapping into my own struggles, too, you know. My struggle to keep on when stuff gets me down. Not just with my stuff, but all the stuff I'm seeing in the community. People I know, who I eat with and pray with. They are really struggling with problems and can't find answers. There's so much misery and frustration and downright evil out there. It can become blinding and stifling if we don't keep our eyes on Christ's way forward. Even if that means a way forward through what is clearly a very deep sea. When you're facing the sea, that's the choice Live or die."

Melissa sit quietly for a moment, thinking. "I like that you're blunt," she finally replies. "It pisses me off, but I still like it. All I can see, though, is loss. Loss of something good, like I said. I don't know that I'm turning to some evil. I don't have a promised land in front. I already had one where I was."

She stops, a tear runs down her cheek. She wipes it off with a brown paper napkin.

"My hope was taken away. My best part of me. I lost that. You had a way forward."

"You see that now," Larry replies. "I see that now. But I didn't see that then. All I saw was a surfboard I would never ride again. All I saw was my wheelchair that wouldn't go on the beach. I'd never ride a motorcycle. All my friends trying not to be jerks but realizing they had nothing in common with me anymore and didn't know what to do with me. I was totally alone, except for my parents, and hadn't anything there. I understand more than you realize."

"Where do I go then? What do I do if I don't want to be 'all Vichy'?"

"Do what God said to the Israelites. Move on. You've cried out. I've cried out. We all have cried out. Reality is what it is. So move on. You weren't wrong to get out of that life your parents expected of you. You were finding yourself. You're not done. There's more. You can be more. You can find something deeper, more creative. You can fight and see what happens. Not against God, though. That puts you back in the arms of the Egyptians."

"Fight who, then?"

"Fight what you see as your reality. Fight the Red Sea. Or rather move on through it. Let God fight it. See what is on the other side of this."

"I just don't know how."

"I know!" L:arry says. "I know!" He hits the table with his fist the second time he says it. "I know that you're in this place where you think it's your right to be bitter, to be mad, to lose heart. You're in a place where it seems natural to stumble in faith. Who wouldn't, right? Who else has to deal with what you're dealing with? At least I can blame my own youthful stupidity. You can't blame anyone except that guy who shot you. But if you hold onto that, if you embrace what you feel you are allowed or owed, you'll never move on. You'll instead be comforted by your frustration. That's a bitter, bitter cup to drink from. The longer you sip the harder it is to put it down."

"So I should just go back to pretending? To being little miss happy Melissa sitting nicely and playing the good Christian girl?"

"No! Not at all. See, that's where you're stuck. Right now you can only see the choice between being bitter or hopeless and being fake. There are more options than that."

"What?"

"Moving on. You don't surrender to the Egyptians. You don't drown in the Red Sea. You move on."

"But what does that mean, Larry?" she asks, sitting up straight and then leaning toward him. "Practically. Don't give me platitudes."

"Sorry if it seemed I was handing out platitudes," Larry replies, and sighs. "Only they're not platitudes for me. They're my reality. When I wake up. When I go to bed. When I hope there's going to be some easy way to open the door so I can get a cup of coffee without too much hassle. When I go to the bathroom. My problems are always in front of me, always sitting with me in this chair. So they're not platitudes for me. But I get how they might sound like it. What's the practical answer? Don't give up. That's practical. Don't lose your dreams. Adapt and respond. Let the limitation guide your creativity. You have to look deeper now. Just as the Israelites had to look deeper in order to find the land of the promise."

"What does that mean for me today? What do I do with that?"

"Go to your physical therapy appointments. It will make a difference for your mind if you do what you can. It's a choice, a positive choice. I didn't get my legs back, but the time I spent in therapy—sometimes agonizing time—got my brain moving. I wasn't a victim anymore. In the middle of it I started thinking not only about my legs, but about my interests, my hopes, how I could help, who I could be. I began reading a lot while in waiting rooms, reading *Sports Illustrated* at first, then news magazines. I became a news junkie—online, television. I realized I was forgetting my issues when I wrote and talked about all of it. I began reading history books, bringing them with me. I read about all the founding fathers of this country, the country my parents sacrificed their whole past to live in. It moved me. I moved on. Across the Red Sea."

"If this conversation was in one of those books sold in Christian bookstores, and I was one of the characters participating in the conversation, I guess I would reply by saying how I've suddenly seen the light, and have a whole new outlook on things. But I don't see that yet. I'm trying to figure out what this all means, means for me. I can't paint. I can't sculpt. That's my income, Larry. When the works I've done are sold, there won't be more replacing them. So what then? Teach? How do I do that if I can't model it? I became an artist because there's nothing else I want to do, or could do. You had this door open. You had the Red Sea part, so to speak."

"You don't get it," Larry says. "You're scrambling around for an answer, an explanation, something that will make this easy. It's *not* easy, Melissa. It's not. Anyone who says 'just smile and believe' hasn't been through anything. They don't know what it's like to live. Let me be blunt again. You say you're not important. But every day I talk to people in the community who don't have anyone. They don't have family. They don't have supporters. They barely have themselves. They live on the streets; some of them with some pretty nasty realities in their life. HIV. Schizophrenia. Whatever. They are the castoffs. The ones who make it—and certainly not all do—are the ones who get what I'm telling you right now. So don't say you have it worse than them. Or worse than me. There's only one difference. And it's a big, big one that a whole lot of people never get over."

"What's that?" she asks, beginning to be annoyed by the lecture.

"It's happening to you. This is your thing. This is your reality. We're good about seeing God's work in other people's lives. We see their struggles in a perspective of hope. But our struggles? They're big. They're looming. They're the ones we not only see but feel in the depths of our whole being. We see the sea in front of us, or the mountain, or the desert, or whatever. It's our legs that don't work now. It's our dreams that are dashed. It's our hopes that are lost. It's our relationship with God that's in question. It's our faith that is at a crossroads. Our faith is perfectly robust when it's other people dealing with issues. But when the challenges are ours—real, life-changing stuff, not introspective, existential crap—we have a stark choice."

"What choice? To have an arm that works or not?" Melissa's voice is clear and sharp.

After a short pause she continues in a more mellow tone. "I made a whole lot of choices that put me on the wrong side of everyone, because I thought I was following God. I made the choices again and again. I lost church friends for being an artist. I lost artist friends for believing in Jesus. I took a stand. And I got shot."

Larry tips his cup back and shakes it a little as he holds it there, trying to get the most of out of the cup. He puts it back down on the table. Plays with the lid a moment. Melissa watches him, leans back in her chair.

Larry smiles. Just a quick flash of a smile. He looks outside. Looks back at Melissa. Then he smiles again.

"There's a point we come to," he says. "A point that sometimes God initiates. Sometimes evil brings. Sometimes we bring on ourselves, out of choice or out of stupidity. Doesn't matter. It's this point that God makes into a crossroads. We're stripped of everything. All we've depended on. The sources of strength we had. The particular parts of ourselves we thought were our foundation. It's burned away. It's what Jesus said when he told the rich young ruler to sell all he had and give it to the poor. It's our thing. It's our stark reality that is our particular loss—our particular emptiness. God takes those moments and makes us choose. We have nothing in front of us to give us a reason to choose to trust him. And we have a lot of reasons—our past, our present, rampaging Egyptian armies intent on our perpetual slavery—to give up on him whether just in our actions or altogether. We have this moment. Time stops. Our past stops. Our future waits. God gives us a choice. Do we believe in him or not? Do we have faith or not? Have we ever really had faith, or were we just thinking there were benefits to a certain lifestyle? What do we do in that moment when there's nothing else except us and God? That's your choice, Melissa. That's the choice of anyone who moves past a young, immature faith and starts becoming mature. The Red Sea is the marker. What will you do?"

"I don't know what to do," she replies. Then becomes quiet. Larry doesn't say anything. After a little while Melissa says, "I don't even know what to think. I'm not sure I believe it, to be honest."

Larry picks up his cup again, and puts it down. He picks up his Bible off the table, holds it a moment while looking at it. Then twists and puts it into the bag that hangs behind his chair, zips the bag shut with an awkward tug. He pushes back from the table.

"I've got class to get to," he says. "Thanks for talking. It was good for me to say this, even if it was just to remind myself."

In fact, though by this time you ought to be teachers, you need someone to teach you the elementary truths of God's word all over again. You need milk, not solid food! Anyone who lives on milk, being still an infant, is not acquainted with the teaching about righteousness.

(Hebrews 5:12-13)

13

when milk is not enough

"Does this mean you're leaving?" Rachel asks.

"Yeah, I think so," Nate replies. "Maybe not right away, especially since I don't know exactly what's next. But I feel like something is next, and it's not here. So what do you think? You didn't answer my question."

They sit at a table on the corner of the outdoor patio at the Columba. The morning's downpour has calmed into a slight drizzle. Not far from them, the water drips off the overhanging awning. They decided to talk out here when a crowd of college students came in for a late lunch. The sudden crowd wasn't particularly noisy. It just seemed more fitting to have the increasingly serious conversation outside on the patio that most people had abandoned for the pub's heat. This third damp day in a row seemed to offend most people.

"Do I want to take over? Not really, Nate."

"That's not actually what I was asking. I'm not handing you the crown. I'm more asking if you would step up in some of the leadership roles."

"'Step up in leadership roles,'" Rachel repeats, and adds a laugh after a moment. "Is that postmodern speak for becoming the new pastor?"

Nate laughs. "You know what I'm talking about. You would fit into that role. Exactly what people need. You seem to have a passion for what is going on here, maybe a vision for what comes next."

"What comes next is I'm going to the supermarket to pick up some food and then off to pick up the kids from school. That's my vision for the future. I don't think that would be an enticing announcement on the Web site, however."

"So you're not interested?"

"Nate, I'm totally interested in doing whatever I can for people in this community, for anyone who is interested in God, and doing what God is asking me to do. I'm not interested in somehow facilitating you wandering away to some greener pasture, just because things seem dry here and you've somehow lost your 'vision.' You want me to be agreeable to that. I'm not. If you leave, I'm staying and I'll be who the Spirit is leading me to be. But I'm not going to participate in some transition that you're manufacturing. You want to leave. Bear the burden of that."

Nate doesn't reply right away. He sighs, looks around, watches the water pooling across the street near a storm drain. Then he smiles and starts to get up. "That's fine. I'll figure something out."

"You know," Rachel says, adding a laugh that seems more like a sign of decision than a bit of fun. "I think I have two more things to add. First, I'm not going to be agreeable to being the new pastor—whatever you call it—and second, I'm not going to help ease your leaving. And I'm going to tell you exactly why I think you're wrong. Three things; I'm going to do three things."

Nate sits back down.

"I was just talking about the future, I didn't expect the Spanish Inquisition," Nate laughs.

"Mike has been exposing me to all kinds of high-class culture," Rachel laughs, and then takes a drink of water. She wants to say what she has to say but it makes her more nervous than she's showing. "It's just that...." She stops, and takes another drink of water.

"What? You haven't said anything about my plans before this. I'm not surprising you with this stuff. So why the change of heart? I want to hear."

"It's not a change of heart. I hoped you'd see what I'm seeing, on your own. I don't like to impose myself."

"Really?"

"Oh, I do it," Rachel laughs. "I just don't *like* doing it. With the Scripture we've been going through, I hoped you would see it. It became more and more clear to me."

"What became clear?"

"That you're still in the middle of your own exodus."

"I thought you were implying I shouldn't go."

"That is what I'm saying. Only I'm not saying it right."

"Let me be more clear about my perspective then," Nate says.

"Alright," Rachel says. "That might help me gather my thoughts too."

"When I was at the other church, working all the time, doing what I thought was God's business, it really became a slavery for me. I had to spend a lot of time doing things that had no real benefit other than fitting into a culture. I was making bricks. Sometimes with straw; sometimes without it. There was vacation time and days off, supposedly, but it was pretty clear people paid attention to when others arrived and when they left, and how much time they took off. It was allowed, but it wasn't approved. Know what I'm saying?"

"I'm following."

"So I began praying. Asked for guidance. Asked for strength. I was burning out. I brought my concerns to the other staff. They didn't listen. With all that prayer, things didn't get better. They got worse. I got more burned out, more frustrated. More problems popped up. My fiancée left me for the guitar player. You know, typical stuff." Nate laughs and takes a few nachos from the just-about-empty plate in the middle of the table. He eats them and then continues.

"All kinds of stuff piled on, stuff you know about, and then it snapped. I was pushed out, pushed out by the Spirit. I went from this heavy weight on my soul and all kinds of responsibilities that felt totally oppressive to almost suddenly having complete freedom. Those doubts and fears and judgments, they got washed away in the sea. Columba and the Upper Room all came together with hardly any of my own effort. It was so easy. Milk and honey, you know? It's been milk and honey all this time. Now, I feel that pull again. Starting to feel tight in my soul. I want to keep the faith of Abraham. Go when God says go. Because I don't think there's this one promised land anymore. I think that with the Spirit, we bring this milk and honey to all kinds of lands. I have an apostle's heart, Rachel, and I feel that calling pushing me from here to new lands."

Rachel opens her mouth and is about to say something, then stops before anything come out. She tightens her lips and tilts her head, looking at Nate, who would probably say she was looking into his soul. She looks at the table, picks up her glass, and then puts it down without taking a drink. She tilts her head to the other side, just slightly. Then a small smile appears.

"I will sing to the Lord," she says, "for he is highly exalted. Both horse and driver he has hurled into the sea."

"The song of Moses," Nate says.

"The song of Moses. Right after they cross the sea and all the Egyptians are washed away. It's their moment of triumph. The moment of freedom."

She pauses again. Nate starts to think he's supposed to have some kind of insight from this, but doesn't.

"Right. And?"

"And, it was a big deal. Moses was justified, right? He brought them out of Egypt. To the other side. 'The Lord is my strength and my song, he has become my salvation. He is my God, and I will praise him, my father's God, and I will exalt him.' I love those verses."

"They're good passages to hold onto," Nate says, mostly because he can't think of anything else to add.

"That's what I'm saying."

"What? I'm not tracking."

"What chapter are those in?"

"Is it 15?"

"Chapter 15," Rachel echoes, takes another sip from her water, and then continues. "Yes. You felt enslaved by the old system. Not exactly the worst kind of slavery, but I know what you're saying. So you were freed, freed to go on. Freed from the past. Freed to celebrate. You feasted. The Columba worked out. People came with you. People like Mike and me joined up. Then Luke had his article to write. Made a big splash. He and Heather got involved. Freedom was all around. And you know what?"

"What?"

"We all made like Miriam. We danced. That's the Holy Spirit working. We danced like Miriam danced on the shores of the Red Sea. But you know what comes immediately after that? How chapter 15 ends?"

"That's not the end of the chapter? I thought that was the end of the chapter."

"No, there are some added bits after that. They started traveling through the desert. On the other side of the Red Sea, after the singing and after the dancing, there's this big desert. Everyone is fine at first. They walk for three days in the desert, and finally get to a spring. Only the water is bad, and they can't drink it. So what do they do?"

"They complain to Moses."

"The people, just freed from Egypt, grumble and ask, 'What are we to drink?'"

"Right."

"And that's what you're asking. What am I to drink? You feel dry. You're in a desert. You think you've gotten to the land of milk and honey but you've only just gotten past the Red Sea. That's what I'm trying to say."

"So I'm not Abraham, I'm the Israelites?"

"Exactly!"

"And I'm grumbling? Not listening?"

"That's how I see it," Rachel leans back in her chair, and smiles. "Do you have a little while?"

"Now that you're saying what's on your mind?"

"Yeah," Rachel replies, with an excited look in her eyes.

"Um..." Nate says, looking down at his watch. Or rather looking down at where his wristwatch would be if he was wearing one. "I think I have another appointment coming in five."

"Five what?"

"In five? Oh, I meant at five." Nate laughs. "I thought you had to go shopping."

"I can go shopping after. I don't want to pass up a wide open door to say what I think."

"Did I give you a wide open door? I don't remember that."

"You did."

"Well, then who am I to say don't walk through it. But hold on." Nate gets up and walks into the restaurant. Rachel pulls out her cell phone and taps the keys—a text to Mike, her husband, asking him if he could pick up the kids, and adding at the end, "I told him" followed by a smiley face.

"You're looking very pleased with yourself," Nate says as he walks back to the table with a pitcher of lemonade in one hand and a couple of glasses in the other.

"I am. Now sit down. And thank you." She adds that last part after he pours her a glass of lemonade. They make their own lemonade at the Columba—something that regulars have begun to treasure, especially on hot days, which isn't what this is. But it still tastes good and adds a little conversation help.

"Vitamin D," Nate says. "Good for us in this cloudy weather. I'm starting to feel it. So, go on and lay it out."

"I got my Bible out. I've collected my thoughts. Now I'm ready."

"Is this hard?"

"It is. I hate butting in. But it's so strong on my mind. I've seen all this stuff so, so much in recent weeks. It pushes me past my usual 'live and let live.' Mostly, I think, because as I've studied this all it has so clarified my own life. Everything came into perspective, Nate, and Mike and I have been talking a lot about our past because of this—more than we've done before."

"And how is that feeling?"

"Hard. I'll be honest; it's hard. But healing. We're at this point where I think it's important. But this isn't about me." She gives a slight nod to Nate, and a smile, showing she's onto his usual conversation-turning techniques. "What it is about, I think, is more of what you've been talking about, what we've all been studying. We don't know how God works and we get surprised by things that happen. Only what God is doing seems pretty clear in Scripture."

She pauses, thinking maybe Nate will add something. He doesn't. He just waits for her to continue, though he does take the pause to refill his lemonade glass.

"We are always asking the wrong questions," Rachel continues, with a slight change of direction. "That's the trouble with so much theology I'm studying now. It's all asking questions, sometimes very deep questions and often very complicated questions. Interesting questions, but so often I hit this wall, especially recently. I get to thinking about what questions God wants us to ask. And I realize they're not the questions we are good at answering."

"What kind of questions?"

"What you are asking, in part. 'Where do we go?' 'Where is God right now?' 'What am I supposed to do next?' 'Why the wilderness?' 'How can I do this next step?' 'Where's the vision and plan?' We have all these questions. You've said it before—God doesn't always give us the answer. We're left with this one question, and it's the one we can answer, but it's the one we don't want to answer."

"So, the question really is, 'How do we respond?'" Nate asks.

"How do we respond to the darkness and emptiness and problems? To the frustration? To the terror? We're not given an explanation. We're given life and told to live this life in faith. And it seems—seems from this passage—the more we learn this the faster life comes at us to shake us from our stance. Maybe that's why Ephesians 6 gives us all those great images, but ends with, 'just stand.' We just have to keep standing."

She takes a drink from her glass and mostly empties it. Then continues, "I think Melissa is really getting this one area. This is the question she's asking. Maybe not directly or with the Bible verses in her mind, but she's asking this very question. How does she respond to all the mess? Does she stand?"

"She's not coming up with a quick answer," Nate says.

"Neither are you," Rachel quickly responds. "That's all part of the process. We're not expected to grow instantly. Paul gives us a goal and tells us to keep at it: 'Forgetting what is behind and straining toward what is ahead,' he says in Philippians 3. That's how we are supposed to respond. We see in Exodus a lot of ways we're not supposed to respond."

"But it's hard," Nate says. "I mean with the Israelites. We don't get a sense of what it was like to be in that desert, three days thirsty and then discover the only available water is bitter. That's disheartening."

"Especially to live it. We live our own things. You have your frustrations you're not feeling this vision or direction. Melissa has her arm. We've all got something. That's the thing, what you said, the Israelites had an absolute right to complain. They were thirsty! Their kids were thirsty! They were free, but so what? They were dying. So of course they complained. Who wouldn't? We're so judgmental about them."

"We're exactly the same, aren't we? I kept seeing myself as a Moses, leading this community. I'm not Moses at all. I'm one of the people...grumbling." Nate makes a grumpy face and mutters, "Grumble, grumble, grumble."

"And realizing we're doing that is the beginning of wisdom," Rachel says and adds a laugh. She fills her glass and takes another long drink, wondering how her mouth can be so parched on such a wet day. Two sparrows fly in under the awning and poke around under the tables looking for remains from a previous sloppy patron.

"The question isn't about water," Rachel says. "The real question we have to ask again and again and again, is who is God? That's the lesson. Do we stand? Or do we fall aside? And the moment of freedom, the moment we're really in relationship with God, is when we learn how to answer those questions. We can go our whole life—even in the church—and never have to really answer that question or stand with God." She throws a broken chip on the ground, and the two sparrows quickly jump to pick up the pieces. "There's no water. What do we do? The Egyptians are following. What are we to do? There's no food. What are we to do?

"The world, and common sense, says panic and grumble. Run away. Go back to slavery. God is saying something else here, and that's the most profound lesson we'll ever learn. Grow up. It's time to grow up."

"Yeah!" Nate's face lights up with a big smile. "Love it. Grow up."

"Now that I've said it I see it even more. I mean, look at this whole story. They were oppressed, passive, completely unable to manage themselves. All they could do was cry out. They cried out and God heard. God gave them the milk of their freedom. But he didn't just open the gate and say, 'shoo!' He didn't even make it easy. All these miracles then there was still testing and trials and temptations. He was helping them stand up on their own and understand what it meant to choose to have faith, to trust in God, to walk with him and live with him. Again and again they run into a crisis and are faced with a choice. Stand or not stand."

"Believe or grumble," Nate responds.

"That's it. Believe or grumble. It's not like God abandons them. But their patience is tested. Will they be willing to suspend judgment for just a little longer?"

"Until water pours from a rock."

"Or food appears in the desert. They have nothing to drink, God gives them water. They have nothing to eat. God gives them food."

"Too much at first, with the quail."

"Yeah! That's a great part of the story. 'You want to eat?' 'Yes!' 'Then eat! But not too much.' It's all about self-control. They have to provide their own balance—something they've not had to do so far. They eat too much. They get sick. It's all about growing up and learning how to live with God and live in this world in a responsible way."

Rachel picks up her Bible off the table and starts thumbing through it, "All through this story God is giving them space, then reaching back, easing them along. He's stretching them, getting them used to living the life of faith that isn't about being victims of someone else. But instead it's about becoming people of promise who reach out toward the promise and take risks even in the face of absolute disaster." She continues to turn pages. "The water is bitter, throw a little piece of wood in it. There's no food; go to sleep and wake up in the morning, but only take what you need for that day. Trust. It's all about trust and control. Real trust, not merely belief."

"Only they don't learn the lesson," Nate says.

"It's always like that for us too. Sure, God worked in that last problem. Or with that person. But *this* thing—that's too much. Like, here, in chapter 17. They have no water again. So what do they do?"

"They grumble."

"God may have helped all those other times, but they grumble again. It's so easy to have faith in what has already happened. But the test is what is happening now. What is happening next. What is the issue in front of us. Faith is always a future-oriented task, Nate. And I feel like you're saying that God's just not working now so you have to go and do your thing to figure out where he is."

"Should I hit the rock with the staff?"

"I don't know," Rachel laughs. "Maybe that's just what we need to do. Something. Or maybe nothing. Just trust that God knows what you need, what we all need, and he's not going to let you die of thirst. Maybe that's the place of faith. You're at this place again where you're risking your self-identity. It got easy for a little while, things started coming together, you got a lot of attention after feeling so empty for so long. Now it's dry. You're free from all that crap in the past, but now you're surprised to be back in the wilderness. And you know what the wilderness is about?"

"Trust."

"Which is why God is pushing you now. He's pushing you deeper and farther to once again trust. You have these emotional and spiritual issues…."

"Well, I did have my car stolen too and my computer die."

"But you got that back," Rachel says. "The car at least. You can't use that excuse, except as a temporary bother. You did have that, though, I guess, and Melissa has the stuff she's going through. None of it is good or even understandable. But that's not the point. To understand *why* isn't the point. We are supposed to respond to who we know God is. That's the point. Do we or do we not have faith? It's precisely the points at which we don't understand life that our faith comes into focus. Whatever it is. Or isn't."

"I feel like I may have inadvertently stumbled into a sermon you've been writing," Nate laughs.

"I'm serious, Nate," Rachel replies. "This is important stuff."

"I know," Nate says. "Sorry."

"It's serious to me now because I'm starting to see how much this is just the sort of thing we tell other people. I'm seeing my own life as I'm talking too. This is where pastors and church leaders get into so much trouble. They are always telling the other people to face up to life, but then they don't see themselves as part of that same challenge and story. You know? And this staying or going thing. That's hitting me right at that point. Who has that option? You've got all this freedom, this freedom that God has given you, that we in the community have given you, and you're acting like there's this big moral choice. All because for the first time in a long time it's actually hard for you. You're used to being ahead of the game. You're used to being the spiritually mature one."

Nate's leg is bouncing underneath the table, and he fidgets with his unused fork

"I'm not singling you out," Rachel continues. "We all do this. Some people, like spiritual leaders, seem to get a pass though."

"Moses didn't get a pass, did he?"

"Not at all! He seemed frustrated with the fact. But God kept pushing him the same way he pushed everyone. He had more responsibility but he had to keep growing, keep learning."

"You're getting me to think now," Nate says.

"Finally!" Rachel laughs.

"It's interesting that we get to this central moment in the Bible—the giving of the law—right after all the grumbling and everything. I tend to separate these two parts—the narrative and the law. But it's all two sides of the same thing, isn't it? Field work and class work."

"I think that's exactly true. It's all the same."

"I keep wanting to free people from Egypt—free myself from Egypt. I'm good at the freeing part. I'm good at talking to Pharaoh and telling people the name of God."

"We want to keep doing what we're good at doing. Especially if it was hard to learn how to do those things in the first place. You spent a lot of time, a lot of your soul, getting this place moving along. Now, you're faced with all of us at this new place. Of course, it sounds nice to go back to what you know."

"What's funny is that isn't easy. It's not like moving on is simple or no work."

"It might even be more real work."

"Totally."

"Only it's work you're comfortable with. It makes you feel secure and knowledgeable. You know who you are doing that stuff, and you know you can do it. It doesn't take any real risk."

"It's risking everything all over again to start over."

"Risking outward stuff, Nate. Not risking your self-identity. We want to dance around each other—in a frenzy, not a ballet—as we all stumble over each other trying to make ourselves feel valuable and important. Always going somewhere else. Drinking the milk. Like that passage in Hebrews."

> In fact, though by this time you ought to be teachers, you need someone to teach you the elementary truths of God's word all over again. You need milk, not solid food! Anyone who lives on milk, being still an infant, is not acquainted with the teaching about righteousness. *(Hebrews 5:12-13)* Ω

"Some want to keep drinking the milk," Rachel continues. "Others want to keep handing out the milk. Everyone is happy. But no one grows. We all stay at the same level of relationship with God. But God doesn't want that, Nate. He doesn't want that from me. He doesn't want that with Melissa. And just because you went to seminary, led ministries, and started a church, he doesn't want that from you either. He's wanting you to go deeper and farther."

"By staying?"

"Maybe. Seems like it to me. If you want to know my opinion, yes, by staying. Only by staying, I think, will you actually learn more—go past the stage that you're being challenged in. You have to learn about God. Learn his ways. Learn his depths. But instead, you could get totally distracted by all kinds of church-planting busyness and new relationships. But the thing is you'll come around again. What happens when you reach this dryness at the new place? Another leaving, another planting? You never grow, even as you keep so busy. God doesn't want us to go and do, Nate. He wants *us*. That's this whole story. He wants us. He wants us to know him, to live with him. He wants us to stop and listen. He wants us to trust him, especially when there's no reason to. Because by doing that, we let go all our attempts to manage and we begin to live free. It's in this wilderness that we can really live free. There's nothing constraining. There's nothing constraining you now. You're putting all the weight on yourself. Only God is just holding out his hand and trying to teach you, teach all of us, who he is."

"Funny thing. All this time, all these months, I've never seen how Melissa and I are learning the same lessons. It's so opposite on the surface, isn't it? But, it's the same." He pauses, and leans forward in his chair. "Shoot. You're right, Rachel. I need to keep thinking on this. Thanks for screwing up the process." He laughs.

"Sorry," she says, with a smile.

"It's interesting how quickly we can see what is right in front of us with just a few words. What happens next if we're not willing to wait with God or wade deeper with him? This is kind of scary."

"If we don't believe and don't trust, we lose sight of him and fall into despair."

"He has done all these miracles. He has given food and water, at the moment of desperation. He's shown that he shows up. God gives the law here." Nate reaches over and picks up Rachel's Bible, opens it and starts turning pages. "Chapter 19, they get to Mt. Sinai. Chapter 20 we have the Ten Commandments, chapter 21, 22, 23." He starts turning the pages a few at a time. "All the way to chapter 31. We have God saying this is how it's going to be. Lays out how to live, what to do. He tells all about himself in the process, like you said. What's in chapter 32?"

"Tell me," Rachel says.

"In all those chapters leading up to it, God is teaching. All the time in the wilderness so far, God is teaching. Like you said, this really is all about field and class work; God is demanding everyone step up. Chapter 32—this is the scary part, because I've seen this in my own life. Chapter 32, the Israelites are tired of waiting. They are tired of waiting for God to clarify. They're tired of waiting to see the results of their freedom. They are tired of waiting for Moses. They're tired of God. So they give all their gold to Aaron and he makes a golden calf. Do you get that?"

"I'm thinking you're seeing something more than I'm seeing," Rachel says.

"What happens when we're tired of waiting for God? When we don't want to grow up? Maybe some of us go like Melissa. Lose the faith. Others of us take what we have, what we know, and we start making up our own structure, our own worship, our own god. That's what so many Christians do, what so many churches do, Rachel. That's the downfall. We don't get the lesson, we don't want to wait or listen or trust. So we make our own gods—gods of gold or whatever—and we parade around telling everyone that's the god of Israel, that's the god of Jesus. Only we've totally missed it all and are absolute idiots. Religious and well-meaning, but idiots."

"Which is dangerous because if people don't know better they think it really is God."

"So everyone loses, and we're stuck in this immaturity, only we don't know any better. We feed more and more into it, unless we get shoved out by God himself, who loops us around through all of these lessons until we get it. Until we really do believe and trust, not in any old version of God, but in who God really is and what he really wants. I knew that. I mean, I've taught that. Only I didn't see that here. Didn't see this with all my frustrations. Now I feel like a bit of an idiot."

"Join the club," Rachel laughs. "At least you noticed."

"At least I noticed. Though, I think I'm going to drink some bitter water for a bit." Nate laughs. And starts gathering the plates and glasses. "Thanks for this, Rachel. I knew it was right to ask you to step up. I just was wrong to maybe think that was because I was leaving an open hole by going elsewhere. Now, I see it's that I needed you to step up and teach me."

Rachel stands up and they walk back into the Columba, dishes in hand.

"I think I've a golden calf of my own to work on, Nate," she says as they put the dishes down in the kitchen. "We've got to keep working on those."

"For a little longer at least," Nate laughs. "Thanks for being honest."

"Thanks for being willing to hear honest. I'll talk to you later, okay?"

"Sure thing. I'm thinking maybe I'll be around."

Then Isaiah said, "Hear now, you house of David! Is it not enough to try the patience of men? Will you try the patience of my God also?"

(Isaiah 7:13)

14

when cowards take charge

"Sorry it's a bit of a mess in here," Mike says.

"You should see my office," Luke replies. "I can't imagine what it would be like if I could wake up, wander down the hall, and be at work. It'd be filled with all kinds of books and boxes."

"All important," Mike laughs.

"Of course! And right where I need them."

"Somehow, I still know if Rachel or the kids have been in here. Everything is just where it needs to be, even if that defies logic."

"It's the aura of the place," Luke says. "You can feel the energy."

"Right. It's not messy; it's a religious experience. Have a seat." Mike picks up a couple books off the couch and waves for Luke to sit.

Despite his protests, Mike's home office is not particularly messy. A few boxes sit near the large faux oak desk, and the bookshelf isn't entirely organized according to topic and author, but nearly so. A stack of loose papers is on the desk with a large white and greenish rock set on top of it. A coffee cup on a coaster sits near the back edge.

"Thanks," Luke says. "So what are your thoughts about doing a religion column?"

"Honestly, I'm surprised you asked me," Mike replies, as he sits down on the wooden desk chair. "Nate is a little more in the game than I am right now."

"Actually," Luke laughs. "I did ask him first."

"Well, now that makes sense. And keeps me humble. He turned it down?"

"Not at first. Was all for it. Then talked to me on Sunday evening and said he changed his mind. Apparently, that wasn't the only thing he changed his mind about."

"Word on the street is he's staying around."

"Word on the street is your wife had something to do with that."

"That's what my sources are telling me," Mike laughs. "She can be pretty convincing, when she wants to be."

"And when she should be. Heather and I were dreading Sunday because we were sure we were going to have to be all nice and falsely encouraging about his transition to wherever. Big relief. Interesting to see what he meant by staying to go deeper. Practically, I mean."

"Very interesting. Boldly go where few have gone before, I suspect."

"So are you up to stepping into the new opening we have for a local religion columnist?"

"You know, Luke, I'm not sure. I get why Nate refused. It's freeing when we let go of having to say our opinion. I've been free for a while now from anyone caring. I don't know if I want to get back into that."

"You're assuming our circulation is big enough to suggest people would care," Luke laughs.

"I've poked around. You're not doing to bad for yourselves. Actually had a little rise in circulation last quarter, I hear. That's not shabby given the business today."

"We're doing better than I expected, truth be told, so I shouldn't be down. False humility curries favor, I suppose. What are your reservations?"

"Well," Mike says. "Like I said, I'm not sure if I want to jump back into having an opinion. I'm pretty happy outside the world of religion, Luke. Now with a regular teaching job, I'm even busy again. And you know that high schoolers are going to keep me busy, so I don't expect to have too much free time for pondering, musing, and researching."

"I get that," Luke replies. "I'm not asking for you to have a religion beat or do in-depth reporting. More of a weekly musing. Something for our Sunday-morning edition. I feel like we found a niche with my series, and I'd love to keep religion a regular focus. Not making us some arm of evangelicalism, but not acting like religion is less important than celebrity news or vacation tips. Like it or not, Mike, you still have a bit of a name in the religion world and I think maybe you even have a voice that could make a difference in how outsiders view what's going on in all the various directions, good and bad."

"Have you thought about Steve Peeler?"

"Not for this gig. Why?"

"We meet for coffee and prayer a few times a month. He's a sharp, sharp guy. A lot more in tune with what's going on than I am these days."

"Yeah, I've picked that up. Surprised me."

"Because he's a plumber?"

"No," Luke laughs. "Though, I guess that would be more fittingly elitist. Because, well, because I've sort of divided serious Christians into being either spiritual or intellectual. Steve struck me on my first visit as being a very spiritual guy. A prayer guy."

"Like me?"

"Ha! Forget I mentioned the categories."

"That's okay. It's something I'm trying to fix in my old age. If I had been a prayer guy, I suspect I would have been much better facing what God was asking of me. Maybe that's why I'm kind of jealous of Steve. He's going about it from the right direction. I went about it the direction that got me influence."

"Honestly, it's that influence I'm looking for. The byline sells the column, especially at first, and, this is going to sound elitist, but 'a plumber' doesn't sound nearly as potent as all the stuff I could put after your name."

"Christian high school English teacher?"

"You know what I mean."

"I do, and maybe that's why I'm reticent. You're a temptation, you know. Not sure I'm ready for that."

"A temptation?"

"Yeah. Because you make me think that I should get back in the game. I'm an unreliable scout, Luke. I have a lot of background. A lot of experience. But, honestly, I'm not trustworthy. That's why you should go with Steve. He's a lot more like Caleb. More open, more bold."

"Caleb who?"

"Have you not been doing your assigned reading?" Mike asks, with a mock stern-teacher tone.

"Oh, Caleb from the Bible," Luke says, not looking like he felt too bad about it. "I admit I've fallen behind the last few weeks. All those laws, you know."

"The ruin of many an earnest attempt to read through the Bible. It's like starting a marathon with a steep hill. Good stuff, but definitely not easy reading. Anyway, I'm not talking about the law. You know the story of Caleb, right? You, a good church boy."

"He's the Israelite scout?"

"See, you do know Caleb. A good man. I wish I was a quarter the man he was. But I'm trying. A little late—maybe too late—but I'm trying."

"So, how does he fit in with doing a column for the *Clarion*?"

"And you, a reporter."

"What?" Luke laughs. "Not investigative enough for you?"

"Do you have a little bit of time?"

"All day. Today is my day off."

"And you're here doing business?"

"I'd like to think I'm here doing friendship...business is just an excuse to get me off the couch and out of the house."

"Otherwise you'd be spending more time watching your soaps?"

"Something like that," Luke laughs. "So, yeah, I have time. Is it going to lead to an answer?"

"I'm not giving a yes or no, yet. Just so you know. Talking through things helps me sort out the best path. So bear with me. I think out loud, and you're a captive audience now."

"So, Caleb the scout?"

"Ha! Always to the point. Right." Mike gets up and walks over to his desk, and picks up the Bible that is sitting near the flat-screen monitor. He opens it up to Numbers 13 while he walks back to his chair and sits down. He rests his arms on his knees as he leans forward to read. "This is the hinge of the story right here. The pop admittance quiz. Everything that has been taught and shown has led to this moment. We're taken out of the giving of the law and pushed back into the narrative. More hardship, grumbling and salvation. More personal attacks against Moses, apparently for him not keeping the right decorum others expected of him. Then here, in chapter 13 we get to the moment God sees what everyone had learned along the way."

> ▶ The Lord said to Moses, "Send some men to explore the land of Canaan, which I am giving to the Israelites. From each ancestral tribe send one of its leaders."
>
> So at the Lord's command Moses sent them out from the Desert of Paran. All of them were leaders of the Israelites. *(Numbers 13:1-3)* Ω

"These guys weren't just random, low-level flunkies," Mike continues. "These were leaders. These are the guys who were supposed to have learned all the lessons and reflected all the lessons."

"What do you mean?"

"Let me back up a bit. Rachel and I were talking about this the other day—and apparently it's what she and Nate were talking about as well. After the Israelites get into the wilderness, they don't immediately arrive at the land of milk and honey. There's a journey. And God doesn't say, 'Now that you're free, I'm handing everything to you.' God is not a genie, merely wanting to hand out dreams and wishes. He's wanting us, Luke. He's wanting all of us. Not as slaves. As heirs. That's the whole contrast here, and like the first conversation we had. Remember that?"

"Romans 7 and 8."

"Exactly. God is always contrasting slavery and freedom, leading one to another. Here it's literal. Slavery is actually slavery in the Exodus story."

"But doesn't Romans 7 talk about slavery being the law?"

"Now you're getting into this," Mike laughs. "Yeah, it does talk about slavery being the law, but it's not because that's God's plan for it. It's all a process. The law is a marker, a statement of a new reality, an emancipation from one existence to another. The point of the law isn't the law; the point of the law is relationship with God, and when God opens up more access to that, we are to step in. He's leading us—all of humanity—to this restored relationship with him. That's the history of salvation in God's plans."

"Which is why you are going to write a column."

"Not there yet," Mike laughs. "Let's keep walking through this. This story hasn't only been about finding freedom. It's also about what freedom means. And freedom doesn't mean living the high life. Freedom is work, man. Work. You have to work to eat, work to drink, work to house yourself, work to clothe yourself. And your family. Freedom doesn't mean sitting on the couch eating Cheetos and watching 'SportsCenter' non-stop. Freedom to live means taking responsibility and going out to become your own person."

"And that's what God is teaching."

"That's what God taught. Those are the lessons so far. He taught about being just in the law, about living in community with him and with others. He taught about trust in the wilderness, not trusting for a nice raise, or a little attention, or expanded borders or whatever. He's teaching trust at the most basic level—the level most of us have never faced before. Life and death, food and water, existence and nonexistence. Our tests of faith are nothing compared to these. No wonder the Israelites grumbled. But that they grumbled was increasingly a sign they weren't ready to live with God. Not fully. They didn't trust God. They trusted what they saw and what they felt. They didn't grumble about God's willingness, they grumbled about his ability to save them. That's the heart of it. They didn't trust him to be who he said he was: God above all. They grumbled and they told God he's not good or strong enough. Again and again they were tested and instead of believing, they grumbled. You might be better than them, but I'm not."

"You didn't see me at the office yesterday. There was some serious grumbling."

Mike laughs, and then continues. "There are people who live out their lives of trust better than I do, and that's why I'm wary, Luke. And being honest with the fact is part of my own progress. I had to give up being a leader, because I was leading like all these people we read about here. I was a grumbler who led others to grumble. That's the thing, going back to my original point: These guys who were sent off to explore the land weren't young, inexperienced kids. These were guys in charge—teachers, judges, spiritual mentors. These were the guys who were the eyes and ears and voice of the people of Israel. They were responsible. They were the ones charged to know the lessons and pass them on. To have faith. They had no excuse not to trust God. They saw every single thing God had done. They invested in Moses' leadership. They saw what happened on the edge of nonexistence when God stepped in with salvation, despite how things looked. These were leaders in every sense of the word. And so they, carrying the whole perspective of Israel's history with them, go into the land. And what happens?"

> When Moses sent them to explore Canaan, he said, "Go up through the Negev and on into the hill country. See what the land is like and whether the people who live there are strong or weak, few or many. What kind of land do they live in? Is it good or bad? What kind of towns do they live in? Are they unwalled or fortified? How is the soil? Is it fertile or poor? Are there trees on it or not? Do your best to bring back some of the fruit of the land." (It was the season for the first ripe grapes.)
>
> So they went up and explored the land from the Desert of Zin as far as Rehob, toward Lebo Hamath. They went up through the Negev and came to Hebron, where Ahiman, Sheshai and Talmai, the descendants of Anak, lived. (Hebron had been built seven years before Zoan in Egypt.) When they reached the Valley of Eshcol, they cut off a branch bearing a single cluster of grapes. Two of them carried it on a pole between them, along with some pomegranates and figs. That place was called the Valley of Eshcol because of the cluster of grapes the Israelites cut off there. At the end of forty days they returned from exploring the land. *(Numbers 13:17-25)* Ω

"They went," Mike says. "Good start. They went into the land. 'Go forth,' right? They followed the command to have a look. They went out. They came back. They reported what they saw."

> They came back to Moses and Aaron and the whole Israelite community at Kadesh in the Desert of Paran. There they reported to them and to the whole assembly and showed them the fruit of the land. They gave Moses this account: "We went into the land to which you sent us, and it does flow with milk and honey!

> Here is its fruit. But the people who live there are powerful, and the cities are fortified and very large. We even saw descendants of Anak there. The Amalekites live in the Negev; the Hittites, Jebusites and Amorites live in the hill country; and the Canaanites live near the sea and along the Jordan." *(Numbers 13:26-29)* Ω

"'God was right,' that's what they said," Mike continues. "'The land is really nice. Look at the fruit, Moses! But it's not the place for us. They're too strong there, so we'll pass.' They had heard the law. They knew how to set up a tabernacle, how to give sacrifices, what to do if an ox gored their neighbor or if a white patch appeared on their skin. They knew their religion. They knew the patterns. But they didn't have faith. That's the point. They didn't have faith. They knew God but didn't believe in God. They acknowledged God was good for religious stuff, but not real life. Not for actual, practical direction on where they were supposed to go. These guys—the leaders of the people—didn't trust God, didn't trust anyone. They had enough faith for religion—for law—but not enough faith for the promise."

"Except for Caleb and Joshua," Luke says.

"They were afraid. Except for Caleb and Joshua. They saw everything the others saw. Caleb and Joshua saw the good and the bad, they saw all the milk and all the honey. They had learned the law under Moses like the rest of them. But they stand out. Because they had learned the lesson God was teaching."

> ▶ Then Caleb silenced the people before Moses and said, "We should go up and take possession of the land, for we can certainly do it." *(Numbers 13:30)* Ω

"The leaders were supposed to go into the land with agreement and shared community. But they didn't. They wouldn't.

So these leaders—these cultural and religious leaders—were now something else. They were leaders in Israel, but they were enemies of God. But Caleb did something amazing: He stood up and showed courage. He not only showed courage for future battles against giants; he also risked his own immediate alienation and ridicule, showing real faith. He stood up against the false leaders, the leaders who wouldn't lead, and stood up for God, speaking truth and speaking courage. That's precisely who God wants us to be.

"Courageous?"

"A faithful person is marked by courage, not by knowledge or religious behavior."

"Really?"

"Absolutely. Not just here. We see this with Saul and we read about this in Isaiah."

Mike turns the pages of his Bible and quickly scans the text. "Sorry this has become a Bible study...I'm involving you in my thought process, and this is how it moves along."

"It's fine," Luke says. "Mind if I get a drink of water?"

"Oh, that was rude of me not to ask. You want some coffee?"

"No, water's fine. I'll get it."

He stands up and walks out the door. The kids are at school and Rachel is at work, leaving the house empty. Luke returns a minute later with two large glasses of water in his hands. He hands one to Mike, who takes it and has a long drink before standing up and getting two coasters out of a holder on a bookshelf. He hands one to Luke, who picks up his glass off the corner table and slips the coaster under the glass.

"I won't read all of either passage," Mike then says. "But just enough to show what I'm thinking. The first is with Saul.

Saul and the Israelite army are about to go to battle with the Philistines in 1 Samuel 13. They're at the battle, but everyone is afraid. The prophet Samuel said to wait for him, and he'll sacrifice to the Lord. Only Samuel is a long time in coming. Everything looks and feels dark. Saul decides to do the sacrifice himself. A very religious act, right? He's not dismissing God, he's offering a sacrifice to God, because Samuel isn't there. Only right after that Samuel shows up and lays into Saul."

> ▶ "What have you done?" asked Samuel.
>
> Saul replied, "When I saw that the men were scattering, and that you did not come at the set time, and that the Philistines were assembling at Micmash, I thought, 'Now the Philistines will come down against me at Gilgal, and I have not sought the Lord's favor.' So I felt compelled to offer the burnt offering."
>
> "You acted foolishly," Samuel said. "You have not kept the command the Lord your God gave you; if you had, he would have established your kingdom over Israel for all time. But now your kingdom will not endure; the Lord has sought out a man after his own heart and appointed him leader of his people, because you have not kept the Lord's command."
> *(1 Samuel 13:11-14)* Ω

"Saul was afraid of his enemies, so he acted rashly. Then he did it again. And again it was hidden in supposed religious devotion."

> ▶ Samuel said, "Although you were once small in your own eyes, did you not become the head of the tribes of Israel? The Lord anointed you king over Israel. And he sent you on a mission, saying, 'Go and completely destroy those wicked people, the Amalekites; make war on them until you have wiped them out.' Why did

you not obey the Lord? Why did you pounce on the plunder and do evil in the eyes of the Lord?"

"But I did obey the Lord," Saul said. "I went on the mission the Lord assigned me. I completely destroyed the Amalekites and brought back Agag their king. The soldiers took sheep and cattle from the plunder, the best of what was devoted to God, in order to sacrifice them to the Lord your God at Gilgal."

But Samuel replied: "Does the Lord delight in burnt offerings and sacrifices as much as in obeying the voice of the Lord? To obey is better than sacrifice, and to heed is better than the fat of rams.

For rebellion is like the sin of divination, and arrogance like the evil of idolatry. Because you have rejected the word of the Lord, he has rejected you as king." *(1 Samuel 15:17-23)* Ω

"He was told to totally destroy the Amalekites. Everything. No plunder. But he didn't do that. He obeyed in part, but he took some plunder and offered some as a sacrifice, making it seem religious. Only he didn't do it to serve God. He did it out of fear. The first time he was afraid of the enemy army; this time he was afraid of his own people. God wasn't with him anymore after that, even though he was still king for a while. Saul was afraid. He lacked courage. He acted religiously but lacked courage. That's what we see with the Israelite scouts. The Promised Land was right in front of them, but they wouldn't act. They saw the bounty and they saw the danger, but they trusted the danger. They didn't trust God. They didn't have faith."

"How is this relating to your situation?" Luke asks. He doesn't mind that the conversation has become a Bible study, but it's not what was on his agenda.

"Shooting for the payoff?" Mike laughs. "Give me a moment more. Bear with me. I want to read this Isaiah passage first. Then...we'll see. From Isaiah 7. Isaiah is talking to King Ahaz of Judah."

> ▶ "Aram, Ephraim and Remaliah's son have plotted your ruin, saying, 'Let us invade Judah; let us tear it apart and divide it among ourselves, and make the son of Tabeel king over it.' Yet this is what the Sovereign Lord says: 'It will not take place, it will not happen, for the head of Aram is Damascus, and the head of Damascus is only Rezin. Within sixty-five years Ephraim will be too shattered to be a people. The head of Ephraim is Samaria, and the head of Samaria is only Remaliah's son. If you do not stand firm in your faith, you will not stand at all.'"
>
> Again the Lord spoke to Ahaz, "Ask the Lord your God for a sign, whether in the deepest depths or in the highest heights."
>
> But Ahaz said, "I will not ask; I will not put the Lord to the test."
>
> Then Isaiah said, "Hear now, you house of David! Is it not enough to try the patience of men? Will you try the patience of my God also?" *(Isaiah 7:5-13)*   Ω

"The passage goes on to be one of the great messianic prophecies. But that's not my point here. My point is again looking at a king who acts religious but doesn't have courage. He doesn't trust God, but says he doesn't want to test God. He doesn't have courage that God will really solve this crisis, but he wants to appear like he has faith. That's the danger. False faith masquerading as leadership and spirituality. That's what God abhors. That's what God wants to teach us, teach us to be better than that. That's the advanced course in spiritual maturity."

"What?"

"If you do not stand firm in your faith, you will not stand at all. That's what Isaiah said to Ahaz. That's where Saul went wrong. That's exactly what was being taught in the whole story of Exodus. It's not just about God's abilities, God's faithfulness to work. The people are being taught to stand in faith, even in the face of sometimes overwhelming opposition or potential disaster. They are being asked to stand, to obey, to have real faith in real-life crises. That's what Saul, Ahaz, and the fearful scouts didn't have. They had religion, but they didn't have courage. They didn't really believe. They weren't trustworthy. God wants us to trust and be trusted to trust. He teaches that. And that is my point."

"Which is?" Luke asks, and laughs.

"I'm Saul, Luke. That's my reality. I'm one of the false scouts. I had my moment, and I didn't have real courage or real faith."

"I thought you were bold in all the stuff you did—the crusades, the organizing, the politics, the public involvement."

"Looks like it, didn't it? And it felt like it. God gave me a church, and a large group of people to help mobilize. With that many people I had a huge voice in my community. I had power. I had influence. That influence spread. With all that power and influence I felt like I never had enough. I had to make use of it, you know. I had to help all those people feel part of something, to define themselves with a cause. What was my cause? All those crusades. But what were all those about? It was me saying culture was too strong. We had to protect ourselves. We had to hide and shield and retreat into our little shell, taking a stand against the world, because it was dangerous and evil. More than that, it was me telling the whole Christian community that the world that was arrayed against us was stronger. So we had to attack, and denounce, and use the weapons of the world. It wasn't faith, Luke. It was fear. I've started to notice how prevalent this is. Whole churches are formed on fear. We're called to hope, but we so easily fall back into responses based on fear. You can see it and hear it all through religions. It's the leaders who won't share power. It's the leaders who spend all their time denouncing rather than empowering. It's the leaders who attack their congregations for being consumers or sinners or for never living up to some supposed standard."

Before he ends that last sentence, Mike starts coughing. He reaches over, opens a drawer, and pulls out a cough drop. "Sorry about that," he says as he unwraps it and tosses it into his mouth. "This dry weather gets to me if I am talking a lot. I go through a bag a week at school. Where was I?"

"Leaders calling for people to live up to standards," Luke replies.

"Right. Don't get me wrong. I'm not saying that calls to holiness are wrong. Those are so, so needed, but we don't need the restricting kinds that negate people, that create these very narrow boundaries that a pastor or leader or whoever can then patrol. It's the people who are afraid of sin who are slaves to sin, you see. Like the Israelites they see giants and are afraid of them, and shrink back and then go out and spread lies about such things being threats to God's kingdom. They don't trust God. They don't trust God's people. So they hide and make it seem theologically correct to hide. They create hierarchies to secure power and hide behind the walls, so afraid of poison they won't drink the milk or eat the honey, and won't let anyone else either."

"So, you don't see yourself as courageous? Is that the issue here?"

"We can look like we have courage by doing it our way. But that's not real courage. Real courage, real faith, is living God's way, the way of freedom, the way of promise. The way of hope. We can make all kinds of religious practices and liturgies and organizational structures and vision statements and mission plans all based on our fear—our fear that God's not going to show up and everything is up to us. Or based on our fear that God *is* going to show up and we won't be in control of anything. We want to satisfy our ego, which we falsely call God. So all my crusades were based on my ego and people's fears, and, well, that had great success for a while, but it wasn't part of the Spirit's work. The more I pushed the farther away I got from really hearing the Spirit. It affected me, even though it was such a slow process I would have sincerely told anyone I was following God's will. God's will was elsewhere, so I fell into temptation. I tried to make my own path in the wilderness. God said no. And I lost everything."

"Where does that leave you?"

"Where does that leave any of us? I talked about leadership stuff. But it's also a lot more subtle. How we live, where we live, how we worry about all parts of our lives. God tells us not to grumble and worry. But we see all the giants in the land and we retreat, and hide, and move away from being open in community and open with God. We don't trust him to be the guide of our participation in this world. We give him part—show up on Sundays or read our Bibles—but hold back the heart of our lives. We don't let go of our fears. We box up our faith and put it off to the side where it won't have a dangerous influence."

"But where does that leave you?"

"It leaves me in Numbers 14."

"Which means what?" Luke replies. He notices that he has been bouncing his knee slightly, his impatience showing a little bit.

"Numbers 13 ends with the leaders being cowards. But more than cowards," Mike responds. "They not only are afraid to take on what God is asking, they start spreading rumors.

They say the land is bad, it's all impossible. They lead—essentially—a rebellion against God, all while sounding the most responsible and attacking those who say otherwise about them. They make the people fear rather than hope. Never trust anyone who brings fear into religion—it's the surest sign they aren't walking with God. God said, 'Don't fear' and the people feared. I, too, was afraid. It's my tendency to pander to people for power and influence. I play the good son, the good husband, the good pastor. It's all a role based on everyone's expectations. When God said go—as I now know he said to me in certain ways while I was a pastor—I ignored him. I made an issue out of distractions and obsessed over minutiae. It kept me busy from hearing and doing what God really wanted me to do, which was a whole lot less public and exciting. We all do that—those of us who are afraid. It keeps us busy. We think we are religious but we're saying, 'It was a lot nicer back in the day, back in Egypt land.' And you know what happens?"

"What happens?"

"We fail the moment. We get overtaken by time. We haven't learned what God is teaching through the time in the wilderness, and so we can't live up to who he is asking us to be."

"What's the lesson?

"You have to learn to trust God and then you have to learn to *keep* trusting God. That's the huge, huge lesson of spiritual maturity and one that God is insistent on teaching."

"The lesson of the wilderness? Trust in God?"

"Have courage and trust in God. It's a lesson we learn only when we face the void between existence and nonexistence, when we are faced with the loss of everything and the gain of everything. Where we are asked—with everything we once knew stripped away—do we, or do we not, really believe in God? We are to show this by our actions, not our testimony. God may not make those moments, but he uses them. Do we really trust God and do we have courage to follow him? That's the question at the entrance of the promised land. And that's why, as I'm thinking, I can't write the column."

"Okay, I so don't get that connection."

"Numbers 14, Luke. I said that, didn't I?"

"Yeah," Luke laughs.

"I better get to my point then," Mike says. "In Numbers 14 the leaders have rebelled, and the chapter starts off with this."

> ▶ That night all the people of the community raised their voices and wept aloud. All the Israelites grumbled against Moses and Aaron, and the whole assembly said to them, "If only we had died in Egypt! Or in this desert! Why is the Lord bringing us to this land only to let us fall by the sword? Our wives and children will be taken as plunder. Wouldn't it be better for us to go back to Egypt?" And they said to each other, "We should choose a leader and go back to Egypt." *(Numbers 14:1-4)* Ω

"Moses and Aaron fall face-down in front of the people," Mike continues, "as they did with Pharaoh. Only they aren't pleading with the people, they are pleading with God not to get dangerous on the people. Caleb and Joshua, who are the courageous men among the people, tear their clothes and mourn. But the people are afraid, afraid of this new looming disaster just like they had been afraid of all the previous looming disasters. They are about to stone Moses and Aaron, condemning anyone who doesn't feed their fears. That's it. They miss the moment. They fail the test. God gets mad. Threatens their destruction. Moses pleads with God to save the people, for the sake of God's name—he argues that all the nations are watching and that God should save Israel because of the promises made, or else it will look like God is not able to win the day. But still…reality hits.

God's reality. He tells the people they are to turn back, go back into the wilderness."

"And so they wander some more, right?" Luke asks.

"Not at first. And this is the point that hits me. They finally, finally realize they've gotten God mad. They've seen his anger finally. He doesn't coddle them anymore. He was gentle at first. He whispered to them that they should trust, while speaking loudly to Pharaoh. He understood their doubts, and stepped in during their crises. But they didn't learn to trust. They didn't learn to have courage. He continued to work, bringing water out of rocks and food out of the sky and victory over armies along the way. But his anger was rising all the while. He whispered, 'trust,' then he spoke it louder, then he was stern about it, and then he started yelling it. And when God yells, there's no mistaking the fact. So the Israelites know God is mad and they decide they want to go ahead and try out the command to invade the land. Only the moment has passed, you see. Time has overtaken them. They showed they didn't trust and they didn't have courage. Once again they followed fear, this time their larger fear of God. They tried to attack the Amalekites and the Canaanites in the land, to prove something to God. They got whooped. God wasn't with them. He doesn't want sacrifice, he wants obedience. He was pointing them back to the wilderness."

"Because they had to learn the lesson of trust and courage."

"Had to learn it. Had to breathe it. They had to trust in God, trust in him and have courage to follow him. But that took going through the loop again. They couldn't just jump in and act like nothing had happened. It had to be with God's timing. And that's finally my point."

"Hooray!"

"Ha! My point is that I was a cowardly scout, and God pushed me back into the wilderness. Writing a column seems like my re-entry into the public world. But I'm not ready for that. I'm still learning. I have a lot more trust and a lot more courage than before, no doubt about that. But I'm not going to jump ahead and try my own timing. I'm in this wilderness time again, and I'm learning. But I want to make sure I really do learn, and really do trust, and really do let go of all my fears before I step back. You know why?"

"Why?"

"That's the scary thing about the wilderness, Luke. There's no guarantee a person will come out of it the second time."

*"In the desert prepare the way for
the Lord; make straight in the
wilderness a highway for our God.
Every valley shall be raised up,
every mountain and hill made low;
the rough ground shall become level,
the rugged places a plain.
And the glory of the Lord
will be revealed, and all
mankind together will see it.
For the mouth of the Lord
has spoken."*

(Isaiah 40:3-5)

15

when a friend walks away

Nate wakes up early and hears only the occasional song of a mockingbird rather than the usual steady traffic. A car horn may have awakened him, but he's happy about that. Because he's up early, he can dedicate a few hours to prayer, with no interruptions. It's a good habit to cultivate; didn't Jesus get up before dawn to pray? Recently he's begun to realize Jesus likely also went to bed fairly early. He thought it funny he assumed he had to sacrifice rest. Nate had gone to bed early last night. Now he's up and praying. And writing. Not really a journal, because it isn't about his day or always about his issues. It's an untangling of random thoughts and reflections on Scripture. He considers what is going on with others in his life—sitting with a pen and with God—trying to listen to the Spirit's whisper. It feels to him like he's a teenager once more, yearning for God's presence to lead him the right direction. He doesn't know what that might look like, to be honest. But there is peace in his soul, growing as he learns that he isn't in charge.

He looks outside and sees a puffy cloud in the waning night sky, illuminated by the half moon not far from setting in the west. He's just finished praying and writing about what's been going on, with no real purpose except to better align himself with God, and align his own heart to trust what is going on. It is too easy to jump in, jump ahead, try to manage, try to control. It is easy to lose heart that way. But he's tired of that vacillation. He's tired of getting excited and losing heart, in varied succession. It is time to let go.

Not let go of his home or his community. But let go of trying to manage God's mission. Following the Spirit means pursuing God's mission. Only it is so easy to reverse that and make pursuing God's mission into telling the Spirit what could and should and can be done. And what can't. Even as Nate has known this in his mind, in his intellect, his heart doesn't necessarily follow this guide all the time. It seems God doesn't just want a mind. He wants a whole person—mind and body and soul.

God had been doing a work. Nate had been trying to follow along. Then he panicked. That's clear now. He panicked and wondered if maybe all the frustrations meant he wasn't hearing God, and needed to do something about it. The thought that God wasn't talking got him nervous. But Nate realized that is kind of insulting to God.

For so long Nate thought he knew God. He was reminded, because he knew the lesson already, what it meant to be a disciple. He remembered the wilderness.

It isn't likely anyone will read what he writes this morning. Maybe if he has a particularly nice turn of phrase he might share it with Karl or Debbie or someone nearby. Mostly it is for himself, and for God. It's an offering, a firstfruits of his thoughts and desires and hopes and plans.

This morning he has already written a lot and is now sitting, staring out the window, watching the cloud change colors, becoming duller as the moon sets and the sky emerges into a bluish gray. More birds begin to sing. He doesn't know their voices yet. That is one of his goals—to learn who sings in the early morning.

His personal reading for the day is in Isaiah 40. After a while in which his mind sat blank, emptied of prayers for others and untwisted from the concerns that seek to poke in, Nate opens his Bible and begins to read—out loud to help retain focus and hear the words better.

> ▶ Comfort, comfort my people, says your God.
>
> Speak tenderly to Jerusalem, and proclaim to her that her hard service has been completed, that her sin has been paid for, that she has received from the Lord's hand double for all her sins.
>
> A voice of one calling: "In the desert prepare the way for the Lord; make straight in the wilderness a highway for our God.
>
> "Every valley shall be raised up, every mountain and hill made low; the rough ground shall become level, the rugged places a plain.
>
> "And the glory of the Lord will be revealed, and all mankind together will see it. For the mouth of the Lord has spoken."
>
> A voice says, "Cry out."
> And I said, "What shall I cry?"
> *(Isaiah 40:1-6)*   Ω

Nate stops reading and pauses on those words. He wonders what to cry. What to say. He wants to say so much. But now, he wants to also stay quiet. He remembers back to early in the study of Exodus what God said Pharaoh was going to cry out.

Nate says the words out loud, "They are wandering aimlessly in the land; the wilderness has closed in on them." And realizes that is precisely what he's been saying for so long. Not to others, but to himself, about himself. In saying these words, in holding onto the promise of Pharaoh, the wilderness did become aimless.

Only there was that voice. That voice crying in the wilderness. That voice that announced Jesus and still announces the presence of Jesus. Making straight, making smooth, making whole.

"Which shall I cry?" Nate asks himself. Then he closes his Bible, puts his pen and notebook back on the shelf above his small writing desk. Sits for a moment in silent prayer, thanking God for his presence, especially in the wilderness where so many were wandering aimlessly when they didn't need to.

"I want to be that voice," Nate says out loud, adding an "amen" a couple seconds afterward.

He gets up and goes to his small bathroom to get ready for the day. It's dawn, and the bathrooms aren't going to clean themselves before the Columba opens.

An hour later, Nate is finished with the bathrooms downstairs and is back in his apartment, with cleaning still on his mind. Karl and Debbie are coming over for a little planning meeting, and Nate realizes his own bathroom and the rest of his apartment need some attention. After dumping the contents of smaller trash bins into a large bag, Nate opens his back door to take his trash down to the dumpster and almost walks right into someone.

Melissa stands there, at the top of the stairs, above the small parking lot, looking away from the door.

"Hey," Nate says, a little startled. "Just hanging out?"

"I saw your light was on," Melissa says, turning. "And came by to say something. But then I wasn't sure what exactly I was going to say. So I got stuck here a moment. Mind if I come in?"

As she says that last sentence she walks past Nate, into his small apartment above the Columba, and sits down on the couch. Nate follows, pulls the chair from his writing desk, and sits down.

"How are you doing?" Nate asks.

"I'm doing fine," Melissa answers, responding to the question as small talk rather than a real question. "My arm is the same. Still the same." She pauses. "Anyway, I've been doing a lot of thinking recently and I have come to a point." She stops, crosses her legs, and fidgets with the dark red pillow next to her.

"Do you want some coffee? It's been in the pot for a couple hours, but it's still warm."

"No," Melissa laughs. "I've already had some. I'm actually on my way to another appointment, but I saw your light on and I thought I would stop by now."

"Turning down my gourmet brew? Must be an important appointment."

"I suppose. Anyway, Nate, I came by to tell you," she says, and then pauses again, looks down at her feet and then back at Nate. "I came to tell you that I'm not going to be a part of the Upper Room anymore. I've thought about it and it seems like it's not right anymore. So...."

She fidgets with the pillow again, and uncrosses her legs, looking like she is about to stand, but she doesn't.

"Why?" Nate asks.

"I don't feel comfortable anymore, that's all. I think I need to stretch in different directions."

"Okay."

"That means I'm leaving," Melissa says.

"I got that. Did you want me to try to convince you to stay?"

"Did you want to?"

"I would love to, Melissa. I can't even begin to say how important you are to all of us. To me. You've been an incredible part of what goes on here in so many ways. But it seems like a lot of people have spent a lot of time trying to convince you and I'm not sure I would be able to add anything."

"You could try," Melissa says, with a weak laugh. "It's not you or anyone else. I…I just don't feel like I can contribute."

"It's not you, it's me," Nate laughs. "I know. It's nothing personal, I don't take it that way. I've heard all you've said along the way. I know your heart."

"It's just that I feel so aimless, Nate. I feel so walled in by everything right now. Walled in by…everything. I have to find some space. You know what I'm trying to say?"

"I totally do," Nate replies. "More than you know. But I think you're wrong."

"Wrong? Wrong about leaving? Well, it's been a long time coming and I think it's for the best." She sits up straight and puts her hands on her lap.

"That too. But that's not what I'm talking about and that's why I understand what you're saying. I'd love for you to stay. I think you are a crucial part of what we're doing here, and maybe even more so now because of all you're going through. Only you're not here this morning because I can convince you. You've never played that game, and I don't think you are now. I just hope this doesn't mean you're totally going to disappear."

Melissa stands up, straightens her red blouse, and picks up her small black knit purse.

"Okay," Melissa says, mostly to herself it seems. "I'm not sure what it means now, Nate. I need to take a break from everyone for a while. Tommy and I broke up. Did you hear about that?"

"I didn't."

"We broke up," she says again. "I guess I might be around again at some point—you know me—but maybe not for a little while. Don't be a stranger though. Feel free to check in." She adds a nervous laugh and starts to walk out. Nate stands up and puts the chair back under the desk. Melissa stops at the door and turns around.

"You said that's not what you're talking about—my leaving isn't what you're talking about being wrong. What *are* you talking about?"

"God," Nate says. "Don't give up on God."

"I'm not sure that I am," Melissa replies. "It's…it's complicated."

"It's not, but it feels that way," Nate says.

"Why do you say that?"

"God has hope for you, Melissa. God hopes for you. Even if you can't hope in him right now, he's hoping for you and he's there, will be there. There's hope in the wilderness, that's what the voice cries out. There's hope. You've lost that now, but God hasn't. That's what I meant."

"I don't know if I believe that, Nate. I don't. I just don't believe that."

"That's okay," Nate says. "I do. God does."

A quick knock on the door behind them—the door leading down into the restaurant—interrupts their conversation. Then it opened up.

"You decent?" Karl asks. He walks into the room with Debbie close behind him.

"I'm dressed at least," Nate says.

"That'll do," Karl replies, then sees Melissa there. "Oh. Are we interrupting?"

"No," Melissa says, before Nate can say anything. "Hey, Karl. Hey, Deb. I just came by real quick and am on my way out the door. Talk to you later?" She directs that last question toward Debbie.

"Of course," Debbie responds. "I'll call." She walks over and gives Melissa a hug. Melissa turns and hugs Karl, and then hugs Nate before turning and walking down the stairs to her car. She doesn't look back. They see her wipe her cheeks and her eyes before she gets to the bottom of the stairs.

"Everything okay?" Karl asks, taking a seat on the couch.

"Yeah," Nate replies, sitting next to Karl. Debbie pulls out the chair at the desk and sits down. "Well, no. But yeah."

"It's probably a bad sign I know exactly what you mean," Debbie says, adding a laugh that doesn't quite belie the tear on her cheek.

Give thanks to the Lord, for he is good.
  His love endures forever.
Give thanks to the God of gods.
  His love endures forever.
Give thanks to the Lord of lords:
  His love endures forever.
…to him who led his people through the desert,
  His love endures forever.

(Psalm 136:1-3, 16)

16

when God deals with slow learners

"Melissa told you?" Debbie asks.

"That she's leaving? Yeah."

"She called me last night and said that was her decision. We talked for two hours after that. I was hoping she would change her mind. She seemed to get it, what I was saying. But I guess I wasn't convincing enough."

"It's not about us," Nate says. "We're not the ones to do the convincing. We're here, we've been here. But this is God's work, and it always has been. God will watch over her. And God will teach her, no doubt using the words we helped to say. But, it's not our work."

"You don't sound convinced," Karl says.

"I'm not," Nate laughs. "But I want to be. I believe that's true. So I'm going to trust that God is with her in the wilderness, just like he's been with all of us. We just keep praying. Speaking of being with us in the wilderness…."

"Sorry to interrupt," Debbie says, "but I don't feel like a Bible study this morning."

"I don't either," Nate replies. "But I think I need to go back, especially now, back to what we've been looking at. I need to remember the promised land right now. Remember the hope. Especially now."

Karl leans over and opens his backpack, pulls out a book and a notebook. He opens the notebook and flips the pages until he finds what he's looking for. Debbie turns and opens her purse, digs through it a moment and then opens it wide to look in. She realizes she has already taken out her Bible and it's sitting right next to the purse.

"Sorry if that sounded cheesy," Nate says.

"That's not cheesy at all," Debbie replies. "We do need that hope. It's easy to get swallowed by the wilderness. Especially right now when Melissa is walking farther into the wilderness, walking away from the hope." Debbie's voice exposes her emotion. She reaches down and pulls some tissues out of her purse and wipes her eyes. "Go ahead," she says to Karl.

He looks at Nate, who nods.

"I was thinking about what we talked about last week," Karl says. "About what it means to be in the wilderness again. I wanted to know what that meant. I mean, what did that look like if we try to boil it down to specific aspects? What should we notice? I'm thinking we maybe should frame the gathering on Sunday night around this. Though I'm not sure how to do that."

"Why?"

"Because they aren't nice encouragements. They're the challenges. The temptations. The wilderness isn't a pretty place. Like we all know. It mangles and it kills."

"What did you find?" Debbie asks, still teary-eyed but trying to refocus her thoughts.

"The wilderness isn't an oasis," Karl says. "It's where God trains, and tests. Jesus in the wilderness tempted by Satan; that's not an anomaly. That's part of how God worked and how God works. And it's not a bad thing."

"Temptation isn't a bad thing?" Debbie asks. "Unless the person falls, then it's a bad thing."

"This is how I see it," Karl replies. "Going into the wilderness...."

"Or back into," Nate adds. He looks out the still-open door that leads to the parking lot.

Karl nods and says, "Maybe the 'back into' part is even more striking because it's fiercer. God whispers, then he yells. He nudges, then he shoves, right?"

"That seems to be the way," Nate replies.

"He doesn't let us into the promised land until we've learned—early or late isn't the issue—it's that we've learned."

"Learned what?" Debbie asks.

"Learned to trust when there's no apparent reason to trust," Nate says. "Learn to let go having to force answers to our needs."

"That's what hit me," Karl says. "What are our answers? What are our needs or temptations? God pushes us, or rather we're tested in the wilderness to determine our answers. Not our verbal answers. That's the difference. It's not what we say. It's what we do."

"Faith without works is dead," Nate says. "That's in James."

"God, it seems, tests our faith," Karl says, "to determine who we are."

"Refiner's fire," Debbie says. "'My heart's one desire is to be holy, set apart for you, Lord.' Maybe we could sing that song?"

"Only," Karl says, "that sounds so simple and easy. Is it really my one desire? Really? No. If I had to be honest, I'd say I have a lot more desires than that. This is what the wilderness tests and what it does. It tests and teaches."

"There's no room for religious sentiment in the wilderness," Debbie says.

"Or," Nate replies, "maybe it's better to say there's no room for sentimental religion in the wilderness. We sing and say all sorts of the right things in church, but then go out and stumble beneath the weight of hard times. Do these match up with Jesus' temptation, you think?" Nate stops talking and starts turning pages in his Bible.

"Where is that? Maybe we should look at that this week."

"Matthew 4," Nate replies.

> ▶ Then Jesus was led by the Spirit into the desert to be tempted by the devil. After fasting forty days and forty nights, he was hungry. The tempter came to him and said, "If you are the Son of God, tell these stones to become bread."
>
> Jesus answered, "It is written: 'Man does not live on bread alone, but on every word that comes from the mouth of God.'"
>
> Then the devil took him to the holy city and had him stand on the highest point of the temple. "If you are the Son of God," he said, "throw yourself down. For it is written: 'He will command his angels concerning you, and they will lift you up in their hands, so that you will not strike your foot against a stone.'"

> Jesus answered him, "It is also written: 'Do not put the Lord your God to the test.'"
>
> Again, the devil took him to a very high mountain and showed him all the kingdoms of the world and their splendor. "All this I will give you," he said. "if you will bow down and worship me."
>
> Jesus said to him, "Away from me, Satan! For it is written: 'Worship the Lord your God, and serve him only.'"
>
> Then the devil left him, and angels came and attended him. *(Matthew 4:1-11)* Ω

"Funny," Nate says, though not with a laugh.

"What?" Debbie asks as she realizes she's been sucked into a Bible study she didn't want.

"The verses that Jesus uses here. They're all from Deuteronomy. I forgot about that. Temptations and testing and wilderness—of course Jesus is using verses from Deuteronomy. It's the same story, really, or the same wilderness tests." He stops, caught in a brief thought, then says, "What did you find in your overview, Karl?"

"Okay," Karl says, and he opens up his notebook. "One second...."

"Jesus was forty days in the wilderness," Debbie says. "Israel was forty years overall, right? So, we shouldn't be surprised if we're somewhere in between those, I guess."

"Here it is," Karl says. "I was looking at Numbers, not Deuteronomy though."

"It's all the same story," Nate says, and adds a small laugh. "It fits together, and repeats."

"Wash, rinse, and repeat," Debbie says, also with a small laugh.

"That's the story of the wilderness," Nate responds, laughing a little more. "I like it! Shampoo for our souls."

"Are you kids done?" Karl asks with a smile. "So, Numbers 14 through 16. There's a rebellion against Moses. This is right after Israel is too afraid to go into the land at first, and then after God gets mad they try it anyhow, but totally fail. They don't get mad at themselves. They get mad at the system, God's way of doing things."

"So they are tempted toward rebellion?" Debbie asks.

"Yeah," Karl replies. "Or as I put it in my notes, in the wilderness they are asked if they will join with those who denounce God. Will they reject God and God's work?"

"Which doesn't always mean rejecting God in name. I don't think they did that."

"No, they attacked Moses. They attacked God's method and his choices, but still sounded pious."

"Atheism takes a lot of forms; the worst kinds are those with religious costumes," Nate says.

"That was profound," Debbie teased. "I'm going to write that down."

"I'll autograph it for you," Nate laughs.

"Do you think," Debbie says, her smile gone in an instant, "this is where Melissa is?"

"Yeah, maybe," Nate replies. "I think she has given up on God and doesn't want to fight for the future anymore. She's wanting to be free from God, because she doesn't trust him. But, honestly, I don't think she's *actively* rejecting God. She's not turned her back on God, just lost hope he's there for her. "

"That's what I think too," Debbie replies. "I don't think she's there yet—totally rejecting God. But I see her headed that direction. That's what worries me. She's on a bad road—a road I recognize because I looked down that road. And I've seen what happens to people on that road. They go through more problems and their situation gets worse. And they don't listen."

"Which is why we need to pray for Melissa, and keep praying," Nate says. God is with her, and it's the Spirit who will work in her life."

"Do you think she'll find her way back?" Debbie asks.

"Back to us? I don't know. I think God will keep after her though. He won't give up on her."

They sit in silence a moment.

"So," Karl finally says. "I think, looking at Matthew 4, that Israel's wilderness and our wilderness match up with Jesus being tempted to worship Satan."

"It's not exact," Nate replies, "but there's definitely a connection. There's a desire to do it 'my' way. To think something is too hard, so we jump ahead, and defy God in the process. I think I've been faced with this one myself the last few months."

"And?"

"And I'm thinking I barely scraped by," Nate laughs. "What's next with the Israelites?"

"They're mad. They lash out. It's full of energy and passion though, active disappointment. Then we have Numbers 20 and 21. Back to the beginning, I call it. There's no water. There's a miracle. But it's not the same."

"How so?" Debbie asks.

"Everyone is frustrated," Karl says. "The Israelites, again, complain, showing they've not learned anything, showing why they're back in the wilderness again. But here, Moses complains too. Moses gets mad, hits the rock, and God tells him that because he didn't follow God's exact command to speak at the rock, neither Moses nor Aaron is going to get into the Promised Land. That's harsh."

"But think of it like what we've been talking about," Nate says. "Moses had a lot given to him, and a lot was expected. He couldn't coast. Just because he was in charge didn't mean he could get away with whatever. God pushed everyone forward, even Moses. Because Moses was advanced, he was seen as the person to reflect what it meant to serve God."

"Like the scouts were before," Debbie says.

"That's exactly it!" Nate replies. "Just like the scouts. Moses in this moment—a moment of testing and frustration for him in his leadership—didn't live up to the calling. After all he had seen, here he was acting the part as the leader, but trying to do it his way. He lost his head, and the relationship was at a point where what seems small to us was really a big deal to God."

"He did get into the Promised Land," Karl says.

"No he didn't," Nate replies. "He saw it, but he didn't walk into it."

"Yeah, he did," Debbie says.

"No," Nate responds. "Later we read about Moses not being allowed in. He dies before the people cross over."

"He got in," Debbie says with a growing smile of confidence. "At the transfiguration, on the mountain. He and Elijah met with Jesus. Moses got into the Promised Land with Jesus."

"Nice," Nate replies. "That's so true. He did get there, didn't he? After a bit of a wait."

"After all he did and went through," Debbie says, "it's sad he couldn't get there with the people he left Israel with." She stands up and walks into the kitchen, opens a cupboard, then another one, and then a third one.

"Where are your glasses?"

"Should be a clean one by the sink."

"You only have three glasses?"

"I don't do a lot of entertaining," Nate laughs, then continues. "It does seem sad, I suppose, but God's more about the end of the game than the feelings along the way. Moses didn't lose God. Maybe, in fact, Moses was too scarred to be the one to lead the Israelites into the next stage. After a whole life of constant battles and being in the middle, the frustration broke him. So God made sure everyone was entirely ready for the next leap. What's next, Karl?"

Debbie pulls the water-filter pitcher out of the fridge, pours herself a glass of water, and sits back down.

"Maybe that's what is going to happen with Melissa," Debbie says. She hit a bump, but there are going to be people she is supposed to walk with in the future in a journey that brings her back to peace."

"Maybe," Nate says.

"That's going to be what I pray," Debbie continues. "Because, in a way, that would make this make more sense to me. Bringing the good out of it. I know my time with grieving mothers hasn't explained anything to me, but it seems to have made me ask the question less. Offering comfort is more healing than hearing empty answers."

"And you've brought healing," Nate replies. "I've seen that again and again."

"Not with Melissa," Debbie says. Her eyes look watery.

"You don't know that," Karl says. "You don't know what is a seed that will grow."

"Maybe, but it's hard to see that now," Debbie says softly.

"Just as it was hard for Moses to see what was going to become of the people," Nate says.

"I don't want to lose my chance," Debbie says, with a weak laugh. "I'll keep the faith that God knows what he's doing with Melissa...and me. What's next?" Both Debbie and Nate seem anxious to keep moving through the material Karl has been studying.

"Well, chapters 20 and 21 seem to be about the same core issues we started with. Basic sustenance and provision, and passage along the way. God seems impatient, and has a lot more expectations now."

"The people were expected to learn the lessons," Nate adds, "to see how God worked and have that influence their attitudes and hopes."

"God wasn't treating them like toddlers anymore," Debbie says.

"That's exactly it," Nate replies. He adds in a mock parent voice, "How many times have I told you kids...."

"God got mad," Karl continues. "He got mad at Moses. He got mad at the Israelites, and sent snakes among them, venomous snakes. At first, the Red Sea parted. Now, Edom won't let them by."

"In the story of Esau," Nate says, "who was the ancestor of Edom, we're told *Edom* means 'red,' for what that's worth."

"I don't know what it's worth, but it's an interesting parallel," Karl says.

"Of course, Nate continues, "since the Hebrew says 'Sea of Reeds,' and not 'Red Sea,' I'm thinking there's probably not too much we should make of any parallel."

"Nate, you're such a nerd," Debbie laughs.

"That's why I'm so lovable," Nate replies.

"Or something..." Karl adds. "So, back to the text."

"God was still working, right?" Debbie asks. "I mean, we're seeing God's anger and all these problems, but we're not in the promised land yet, and I know my Bible well enough to know that they do get there, not too long after this."

"That's the thing," Karl says, "and I was going to hit on that later. God is totally working. There are all kinds of frustration. All kinds of irritations. God is teaching fierce lessons and he is increasing expectations. The people fail, they stumble, they fall. But God still works. In these same passages we read about Israel winning key battles. They make progress. Not as quick as if they really understood God, but they are moving forward."

"God was keeping his promise," Nate says. "God was leading them toward the promise. He just doesn't promise it will be easy...."

"Especially if we get in the way," Debbie adds.

"Especially if we don't learn what we're supposed to know," Nate agrees. "But God works still. He's pushing because he's wanting his people to grow, to find the promise."

There's a long pause after this, each person sitting for a moment with that reality, each thinking of their own promise, their own future, and a glimpse of the path that has got them this far.

"Okay," Karl finally says, then looks down at his notes. "Then we have what I call the 'temptation chapters.' The first section I talked about I think was about pride. The people were wrong, but didn't want to be wrong. Pride leads to rebellion. The second section I talked about was desperation, where there were real needs and real problems, which led to grumbling and loss of faith. So in Numbers 22 through 25 there are temptations. There are problems, but there are also new opportunities—ways in which personal choices can point the people to or away from God."

"Such as?" Nate asks.

"Sex and power," Karl replies. "Balaam is hired to curse Israel. He's a prophet or holy man or whatever. Only he can't do it. This guy—this guy who isn't part of God's chosen people—apparently has this understanding that God isn't someone to mess with. This person outside the fold has more respect than those inside. He's offered power, and no doubt influence, but he won't do it. In fact, he does just the opposite. He's tempted, and he becomes this person who hears God and listens."

"Isn't he the one with the talking donkey?" Debbie asks.

"Yeah," Karl replies. "Balaam fights temptation, and then is given this potent reminder to keep doing so, to keep fighting."

"He's our help in time of troubles," Debbie says. "Even if that help seems to make it more frustrating," she adds, with a small laugh.

"That's right," Karl laughs. "So things go well for Israel. They aren't cursed, they're blessed. Everything seems fine. They are in a place where there's food and there are women. Temptations. These aren't evil because of themselves, as I can tell...."

"That's a relief," Debbie adds.

"...but they are bad because they are temptations to depart from the focus on God. They've been given the law not too long before, but it's been hard. Life with God hasn't been easy. God has discipline. His goal isn't to make us happy; his goal is to lead us to maturity—like we've talked about a lot. God ordains feasts, but also fasts, discipline and training. A life in the wilderness can be totally frustrating. So when there are others around—others doing good, eating well, free to live as they want—it's easy to ask what's the point of following God. Take the easy way, as it doesn't make a difference."

"Or makes it easier in the moment," Nate says.

"Or makes it easier in some way, that's right. The Israelites—not all of them but a lot of them—gave in. Indulged. They were tempted by the sex and stayed for the sacrifices. It was a gateway. They worshiped other gods. They didn't hold onto God. They rejected him because they wanted to focus on themselves instead of on God. And they got burned."

"Things became good and that became a problem," Debbie says. "The wilderness is a dangerous place—rebellion, desperation, temptation."

"Oh my!" Nate says, with a chuckle. "What we have to remember, and make sure people pick up on, is that this isn't because God had rejected Israel. These aren't the judgments the prophets talked about; that's what I'm finally seeing. All this stuff, all that happened, all these choices are coming about because God led the people into the wilderness. This is, in essence, all God's work because he's leading them to this new freedom, this promised land. But they all have a choice in the midst of it."

"We think God is this outside force, aloof, and we lose heart," Debbie says. "We lose sight of God who is with us in it, who helps us."

"Because he walked the road too," Nate adds.

"*With* Israel," Karl says. "Not against it."

"Not just with Israel," Nate says. "This is all the story of the gospel. Jesus endured it all. We don't see this magical life full of blessings and great honors. We see struggle. Death. Torture. A lot of joy and wisdom along the way, too, but a lot of coming face-to-face with the reality of the world's evils. Jesus faced it all, the same way we do, only with a perfect faith. So it's not like we're asked to do something God doesn't understand. What's the verse in Hebrews? 'Because he himself was tested by what he suffered, he is able to help those who are being tested.' God is with us in the wilderness, because he has spent a lot of time there himself. So there is our hope. Even if there's all kinds of dangers too."

"The wilderness isn't defined," Karl says.

"What do you mean?" Debbie asks.

"It is what we make it, I guess we can say. God moves. God works. We're asked to have faith, and the wilderness is where this faith becomes real and alive, or where it is shown to be empty and a mist."

"Our faith defines it, in a way," Debbie says, with a hint of a question in her tone.

"That's the place of maturity," Nate says. "God takes this risk with us. His name is on the line. We see it all through this story. And we're asked to put our lives on the line too, taking risks that God is who he says he is. That's the thing about all these temptations and whatever we're talking about: It's easy to look at people dealing with those things, look at ourselves when we deal with those things, and think they are present because God is absent. But that's so not true. God is never absent. Those moments might be coming precisely because we're on the border of the promised land and are being asked, being tested, being trained, to go to this next place of hope and peace and maturity. I remember reading about John Wesley. Wesley said that after his great conversion experience he began experiencing more temptations than ever before; more lust, more temptations in every direction. He was freed, but he was freed to make the kind of decision for God with all his life—tested in fire and frustration, I suppose."

"So what do we do with this?" Debbie asks.

"For our gathering?"

"That's the question we're supposed to ask," Debbie replies. "Not 'why?' Asking why is the more obvious question. But that's not the question God is pushing us to ask. The question is what do we do with it. What do we do in moments of desperation? What do we do in moments of loss? What do we do in moments of temptation where money and power or whatever are handed to us? Do we forsake God because we don't see him, or because we see something else more clearly in that moment? Or do we have faith?"

"Have faith that God is about winning this whole game," Nate says.

"God wins," Debbie agrees. "God wins, and our hope is in that. The wilderness leads us to our free-will choice of whether to participate on his team or stay on the sidelines, or join the other team. The wilderness is our boot camp, I guess. Awful, but necessary. Necessary for who God wants us to be and necessary for who we can be for others, in their hurts."

"We learn to love God and love others," Karl says. "That's the theme."

"If we choose that," Nate says. "We are given a choice to walk away, like the rich young ruler did—or we can choose to hold on to our faith and let go of that which binds for the sake of gaining that which is better. If we have love, it will be revealed in how we live and respond. We don't need to prove our love is there."

"So what does that mean for our Sunday night?" Karl asks.

"Maybe we should share our own exodus stories," Debbie says. "You could share what you shared here, Karl, and then we could talk and see how God works in all our frustrations and problems. Share our crosses, I guess we could say."

"Put perspective on the hard times," Karl says.

"Not just the hard times. But then again, maybe talking about those is important because that's not what churches 'do,'" Nate says. "Churches want to emphasize the successes, the victories, how one person is better than another. But that's not really it, is it? Those things are not necessarily the sign of God's work. It's the people in the wilderness God is really working in and among, really teaching and training. Maybe we could emphasize that, and turn the world's perspective—that the church so often embraces—on its head and really get at the Scripture. Prosperity isn't the sign of God's work. Sometimes just the opposite is true, because God is playing to win everything, not to coddle us with presents and leave us spoiled children."

"I like that," Karl says. "Just tell our stories—a kind of confession. Not of our sins but of our real lives. I think we know a lot of people's stories, but maybe it would be good to share our stories again, in the perspective of God's victory—talking about God's path to promise, even if some of us haven't even come close to seeing where this will lead us. Thanksgiving without knowing the end. Holding onto the hope, because God has told us there's still so much hope. Might be a way to keep us focused on staying strong, even when we don't see why we should."

"I'd also like to include a psalm I read the other day," Nate adds. "Something that maybe we could do as a liturgy. It has a built-in response, so one person could speak the first line, and everyone follows with the refrain. It's a reminder of God's promise and his work."

"Which psalm?" Karl asks.

"Psalm 136."

> ▶ Give thanks to the Lord, for he is good.
> *His love endures forever.*
>
> Give thanks to the God of gods.
> *His love endures forever.*
>
> Give thanks to the Lord of lords:
> *His love endures forever.* Ω

Debbie and Karl pick up the rhythm and repeat the refrain after Nate speaks the line.

> ▶ to him who alone does great wonders,
> *His love endures forever.*
>
> who by his understanding made the heavens,
> *His love endures forever.*
>
> who spread out the earth upon the waters,
> *His love endures forever.*
>
> who made the great lights—
> *His love endures forever.*
>
> the sun to govern the day,
> *His love endures forever.*
>
> the moon and stars to govern the night;
> *His love endures forever.*
>
> to him who struck down the firstborn of Egypt
> *His love endures forever.*
>
> and brought Israel out from among them
> *His love endures forever.*
>
> with a mighty hand and outstretched arm;
> *His love endures forever.*
>
> to him who divided the Red Sea asunder
> *His love endures forever.*

and brought Israel through the midst of it,
His love endures forever.

but swept Pharaoh and his army into the Red Sea;
His love endures forever.

to him who led his people through the desert,
His love endures forever.

who struck down great kings,
His love endures forever.

and killed mighty kings—
His love endures forever.

Sihon king of the Amorites
His love endures forever.

Og king of Bashan—
His love endures forever.

and gave their land as an inheritance,
His love endures forever.

an inheritance to his servant Israel;
His love endures forever.

to the One who remembered us in our low estate
His love endures forever.

and freed us from our enemies,
His love endures forever.

and who gives food to every creature.
His love endures forever.

Give thanks to the God of heaven.
His love endures forever. Ω

"His love endures forever," Debbie repeats. There is a tear in her eye. "That's the promise. That's the dance. That's the hope and the music and the Land. That's it. That's what we have to hold onto."

"If we hold onto that," Nate says, "in all of life's joys and frustrations—holding to peace rather than chaos even when everything seems dark—we win with God. And we hold onto this the most in the midst of the wilderness, which is God's path to his victory. I hear a voice crying in the wilderness, and it is telling us to hope. God's love endures forever."

www.ingramcontent.com/pod-product-compliance
Lightning Source LLC
Chambersburg PA
CBHW051041160426
43193CB00010B/1031